ONE MINUTE PICKLEBALL

A Smorgasbord of Basic Rules,
Dry Descriptions,
Slanted Perspectives,
Questionable Advice,
& Wry Humor

by

J. Mortswen

(PROBABLE) PRE-PUBLICATION ENDORSEMENTS FOR THE BOOK, *ONE MINUTE PICKLEBALL* (AND ITS AUTHOR)

"This book is going to be a huge hit. *Uge. Really* uge!"
>Donald Trump (U.S. President)

"My grandpa claims he is a descendant of Swedish royalty, but I have my doubts. Uffda!"
>Axel (grandson)

"I'm glad I didn't read this book before I became a championship pickleball player. It would have ruined my game entirely."
>Kyle Yates (gold medalist)

"Do you know that my father goes around placing pickleballs into bird nests and thinks it is funny? (The birds don't)"
>Heidi (daughter)

"J. Mortswen could have summarized all he knows about pickleball into one *minute*, period."
>Anonymous

"My grandpa gives me the best hugs!"
>Pearl (granddaughter)

"I sure hope J. Mortswen doesn't *charge* anything for this book."
>K. L. (*former* friend)

"Maybe now that the book is published the author will quit talking about pickleball in his sleep."
>Diane (wife)

"Does the Texas phrase, 'Big hat; no cattle' tell you what I think about this author?"
>Jerry Jones, (Dallas Cowboys)

"After reading this manuscript, I just wish that my grandfather had a great sense of humor like J. Mortswen does."

Ruth (granddaughter)

"All I see in every page of this book is fake news. Yes, *fake news*. That's all I see."

Donald Trump (Twittering critic)

"Fantastic book. Useful information. Great writer. Love the humor. It's a *must* buy. The author deserves at least a Pulitzer Prize, if not a Nobel award for literature."

Lillian Mortswen (mother of J.)

DEDICATION AND ACKNOWLEDGMENTS

Many people deserve credit for helping me to arrive at my current level of pickleball knowledge and skills—former instructors, clinic leaders, book authors, professional players, YouTube video developers, and dozens of friendly on-court competitors--and I can only thank them as a group.

Special thanks goes to one of the kindest friends with whom I have had the pleasure of both teaching and playing pickleball—(retired) Navy Admiral Donald "Smoke" Hickman. Many years ago he and I unwittingly began the basis for this book by writing a series of weekly admonitions to neighborhood pickleballers in The Villages. We called it "Pickleball Patter," and its anonymous coauthors were "Smasher" and "Dinker." The written products may not have received rave reviews, but we thoroughly enjoyed lending a little humor to some serious suggestions.

Having taught introductory pickleball classes in both Florida and Minnesota for many years, I would also like to give my most sincere thanks and admiration to all of my former pickleball students. Your attentiveness, willingness to learn, joyful reactions, dedication to improvement, and appreciative comments have made the time spent with you highly worthwhile and satisfying. My heart is warmed every time I see indications of your evolving skills on the court!

One particular group I want to acknowledge is the "Coordinating Committee" of the Aitkin Area Pickleball Association. This group (consisting of Mary Beal, Jim Benda, Dorothy Casey, Mike Hagen, David Hommes, Pat and Mark Hodges, and Janet and Rodger Lindgren) has been an absolute delight to work with, and they have provided unbelievable support in so many ways as we have tried to advance the cause of pickleball in the local area. It's such a pleasure when people like these suggest solutions to problems and willingly shoulder responsibility for tasks. They are pickleball heroes behind the scenes, and I value each one of them.

Our group's great appreciation goes to all those persons who so generously donated to the pickleball court fund drive. You have helped make our collective dream come to fruition!

Finally, I wish to give enormous credit to my wife of fifty-plus years. She has graciously lived with a pickleball addict and listened to his frustrations, rants, corny ideas, endless "what if" explorations, and detailed blow-by-blow reports of his highs and lows on (and off) the court. She has also painstakingly reviewed every word of this manuscript and made numerous useful corrections and incredibly appropriate suggestions for improvement. It even brings back memories of the multiple times that she typed on an electronic typewriter (without complaint) multiple versions of my much lengthier dissertation back in 1970. Best of all, she has been a constant source of emotional support and a much-appreciated cheerleader for me throughout our marriage. Thank you, Sweetheart!

J. Mortswen

INTRODUCTION AND OVERVIEW

As you will see from my "About the Author" section immediately following this introduction, I have played pickleball for a long time, attended clinics, watched videos, and read articles and books on the subject. I have also taught numerous classes over the past ten years. Most important, however, is the time I have spent *thinking about and reflecting on* this wonderful game—and how best to share that knowledge and insight with an inquisitive, receptive, and appreciative audience.

I fully recognize that prospective players learn in different ways and at different speeds. Some are like sponges that are receptive and thus willingly soak up any shared knowledge. Others are great questioners, and they wish to know *why* a particular suggestion I make is appropriate. Some have racquet sports backgrounds that can impact (usually positively) their achievement in a new sport. Some learn best by *listening*, others by *reading*, others by *seeing*, and others by *doing* (or by combinations of methods).

The temptation for an instructor or author is to expedite *efficient* learner progress by sharing large amounts of information in rapid sequence, thus demonstrating how "smart" he or she is (at the risk of information overload and recipient confusion, of course). On the other hand, I fully believe that learning is best achieved through providing *small* doses (small bites of the proverbial elephant), supplemented by readily available backup information. Another important ingredient revolves around learner readiness (the internal desire to learn) and self-discovery/self-critique. The readiness factor was captured beautifully in a billboard I saw recently that said, "If you are not willing to learn, no one can *help* you. If you are determined to learn, no one can *stop* you." I'm assuming that readers of this book are already committed to learning more about pickleball.

Some time ago, I chanced to read my astrological horoscope in the newspaper one day. It said:

"You'll never have enough time to impart what you know in great detail. So choosing your stories well and telling them succinctly will be your keys to making sure everyone has understood you."

That is when the idea began for preparing a short book of "one minute" perspectives on pickleball. Rather than add one more book of technical terms and detailed diagrams and sophisticated strategies, I felt that a unique, concise, and readable approach to sharing information would work best. In essence, these criteria produced the idea of a "One Minute Guide to Better Pickleball," since much of the individual topical content gathered* and presented here can be scanned and absorbed in a short period of time (and reviewed later).

Alternative titles I flippantly considered included the well-worn "Everything You Always Wanted to Know About Pickleball, But Were Afraid to Ask," the Shakespearean "Much Ado About Nothing New in Pickleball" adaptation, the egocentric "Collected Wisdom" approach, or the truly boring "Collected Essays of J. Mortswen."** For better or worse, all of those titles were eventually discarded. ☺

This book does not demand (nor do I encourage) reading it sequentially from cover to cover, for it does not flow from beginning to end like a novel, nor have I made any attempt to integrate the material. The reader is better served by selecting (picking and choosing) one or a few specific items of interest at that moment, much as a diner would do at a Scandinavian *smorgasbord*. In that sense, the book is more akin to a buffet of topics or a simple reference manual. Finally, this book has some uniqueness in that I have chosen to address a handful of topics that are seldom included or confronted in other publications (see, for example, my comments on the Ball Hog, Body Shots, Clichés, Pickleball Addiction, Resolutions for Success, Useful Pickleball Excuses, or the irreverent "Common Ways to *Lose* Points").

There is much to debate within the topic of pickleball, and the subtitle I created hopefully reflects the fact that some of the content in this book is simply *one person's perspective*. It is a composite of what I think I know, what I've tried to do (or would like to do), what makes intellectual sense to me, and what has worked for me on occasion (with a bit of humor interspersed occasionally). In that sense, much of the material is written in the informal (casual) voice, wherein I am speaking from my heart and using first-person pronouns to reflect my ideas, and second-person pronouns to connect with my audience. *Readers are strongly encouraged to question the recommendations and explanations, consult other sources, and listen to true experts in the field.*

Chapter I provides a description of pickleball and its background, introduces the key rules and terms, and focuses heavily on safety, etiquette, and hydration.

Chapter II is intended to help the novice player get started. It introduces the serve, the scoring system, the return of serve, basic strokes, and making line calls.

Chapter III introduces a variety of other shots in pickleball—volleys, third shot drops, dinks, overhead smashes, and lobs.

Chapter IV includes discussion of items not in the rules but useful to know—practice groups, pickleball ratings, No Man's Land, getting to the NVZ, the "golden middle," and Unforced Errors.

Chapter V discusses advanced concepts such as teamwork, shadowing, re-setting the point, body shots, bangers, and poaching.

Chapter VI provides a variety of ideas for using a positive mental attitude, conscious strategies on the court, and common ways to lose points.

Chapter VII becomes truly lighthearted (unleashing my "inner self"), touching on pickleball addiction, the infamous "Oh, Oh" shot, the "Benda" shot, clichés, and fun with pickling (such as handy excuses for poor performance).

Chapter VIII concludes the collage of topics with brief treatment of leg cramps, referees, rally scoring, skinny singles, and where to go for additional information.

It has been a labor of love to think about this material and construct the final product. I hope that each reader will find something of value within it.

Good luck, and good pickling!

J. Mortswen

*Note: I have no pretentions that all the thoughts and material contained herein are my own. I have freely borrowed (and usually rephrased and modified) thoughts and ideas from many experts in the field. Where possible, I have attributed the concepts to them, and therefore they deserve the original credit. I have simply sought to identify the most useful material and present somewhat complex ideas in simplified and readable form. Errors and overstatements are my own responsibility, of course.

**Having been a textbook author in my previous career, I always thought it would be fun to adopt a pseudonym (pen name, or *nom de plume*) as a way to remain somewhat anonymous in my writing. By doing so (finally) in this book, I can claim to have joined the ranks of Dr. Seuss, Mark Twain, Mother Jones, John le Carre, and Ann Landers!

ABOUT THE AUTHOR: AN INTERVIEW WITH J. MORTSWEN

What is your work and family background?

I was born and raised in Aitkin, graduating from AHS in the great class of 1960. After receiving my doctoral degree, I taught a variety of management classes at the University of Minnesota Duluth, retiring in 2003 (when we moved back to Aitkin, MN). My wife (Diane) and I have lived in Minneapolis, Tempe (AZ), Duluth, Aitkin, and The Villages (FL). We have two adult children and three grandchildren (who are, of course, brilliant, handsome, personable, talented, and above average in all respects!).

What is a "fun fact" about you that most others don't know?

My first job was in a funeral home, where I assisted the mortician and rode along on ambulance calls in the Aitkin area. It was an eye-opening experience for a teenager!

How did you first become involved with pickleball?

We moved to Florida (wintering there) about a dozen years ago, and some new friends introduced me to the sport. I was overwhelmed at first in terms of my skill level, but was also greatly intrigued by the uniqueness of the endeavor. I began playing pickleball regularly, and learned more each day by playing with and against players who were clearly better than me. I eventually became certified in The Villages as an instructor and trained as a referee. Currently, I often play pickleball several times a week. My wife would report that I am "addicted to pickleball."

What other sports or recreational activities have you played?

Let me be crystal clear—I was *never* directly involved as a player in any competitive high school athletic endeavor. Many years later, I dabbled in tennis, volleyball, wallyball, and golf (but never achieved much success in those areas). In the outdoor realm, I also enjoy duck, grouse, and deer hunting with friends.

Which pickleball paddle do you use?

I've owned several paddles over time, partially because they wear out after a few years and partly because I am always searching for the paddle that will help me play my best. (Paddles differ in shape, weight, composition, grip size, etc., as well as in colors and designs). I recently changed from the "Venom" composite paddle to the Engage "Poach" model that I like because its slightly lighter weight (7.4 oz) and padded grip provide me with a combination of power (paddle speed and force) and control (feel).

Do you have a warm-up routine?

Definitely. Before I go to the court, I do a variety of stretches for my back, arms, legs, and feet so as to help prevent injury. I begin drinking water to hydrate my body and take a variety of supplements to prevent leg and foot cramps. I *always* apply sunscreen (since I am prone to developing skin cancer).

On the court, I try to resist the temptation to begin playing immediately, by practicing a few serves, volleys, lobs, & "dinks" over the net before the game begins. Like most recreational players, however, I can't wait to start an actual game.

What shot do you practice the most?

Since I play doubles pickleball exclusively, I believe (and preach) that the serve is a critical (and relatively easy) shot to make. Although even a good serve seldom causes opponent errors, bad serves invariably cost my team one or more *potential* points. Unless I try to get "cute" and aim too close to the boundary lines, I honestly believe that I can be accurate well over 95% of the time when I serve. The service is also the easiest shot to make, since that is the only time when the ball is not moving toward you from your opponent.

What is the most important shot in pickleball? Why do you believe that?

There are many answers to that question, and they vary according to whom you ask. It could be the serve, the return of serve, or the infamous "third shot drop." Others will say that any shot aimed downward and just over the net (with appropriate pace) is more likely to be a winner, as it will be difficult for your opponent to return it well. Increasingly, I have become an advocate of consistently making almost *any* return shot, which gives your *opponent* a chance to make an error. The idea is just to keep the ball in play, minimize your own errors, and play percentage pickleball.

What is your favorite shot, and why?

I suspect that my opponents would say that I favor (enjoy) making a hard smash of a ball that is lofted softly to me just a few feet above my head. When done correctly, this "slam" can be as satisfying as a long and straight drive off the tee on the golf course. In addition, it can be quite intimidating to my opponents.

Actually, however, I mostly enjoy making a moderately soft passing shot that catches my opponent off guard—especially if they are out of position or unprepared.

What is your greatest weakness (liability) in pickleball? Your greatest strength (asset)?

The first question is an easy one to answer, as it applies to many areas of my life. It is my *impatience*—my foolish desire to end the point quickly without waiting for a better opportunity.

I think my biggest assets are my relatively good reaction time in seeing/meeting opponent shots, along with my interest in self-improvement (via reading pickleball magazines and books, attending clinics by master coaches, and watching videos of champions such as Sarah Ansboury, Kyle Yates, Deb Harrison, and Robert and Jodi Elliott).

What is your current interest?

I am passionate about the game of pickleball, and I thoroughly enjoy being an Ambassador of the sport in Aitkin County for the USA Pickleball Association. In particular, I love to teach new players the rules, various types of shots, and winning strategies. I also enjoy passing on my insights and experiences by coaching existing players as they develop their skills and become more adept on the court.

What is the best advice you like to give to your pickleball students and others?

• Do everything you can to *play safely*, avoid injury, and enhance your skills.

• Keep your *paddle up* (in the ready position) at all times.

• Play hard, but *enjoy the experience* of every game while being a good sport.

• Think and play as a *team*; cooperate and communicate with your partner while complementing his/her attributes with yours. Also *compliment* your partner.

• *Aim* (place) your shots with a target in mind. Remember the "golden middle."

• *Don't overthink* the game (even though I do).

• Make friends, laugh, and *have fun*!

Table of Contents

ONE MINUTE PICKLEBALL
A Smorgasbord Of Basic Rules, Dry Descriptions, Slanted Perspectives, Questionable Advice, & Wry Humor

by J. Mortswen

CHAPTER 1

Explanations, Rules, & Safety

A BRIEF INTRODUCTION TO PICKLEBALL

Pickleball has been described as America's "fastest-growing sport." The number of courts to play on nationwide has increased to over 6,000 sites (in all 50 states) in the past few years, while the number of players has grown exponentially into the millions. The game is played with wooden, graphite, composite, or aluminum paddles (not strung racquets) about the size of table tennis paddles and with a baseball-sized "Wiffle" ball on a 20' by 44' court (the same size as a badminton court, so that there is not much running involved). A net is strung across the center of the court at 34" high in the middle. **Pickleball** can be played as either a singles game or (more typically) as a doubles game. It is fast, exciting, a source of good physical and mental exercise, a chance to laugh at oneself, an opportunity for stress relief, *loads* of fun, a chance to make new friends, and "Yes, it burns calories."

    Pickleball serves are made *underhand* only, they must fall into a defined area of the court (the box immediately in front of the diagonal receiver), and only the serving team can score points. The return of serve made by the opponent is then subject to the "two bounce rule" wherein the serving team must let the **pickleball** also bounce on their side of the court before subsequent exchanges can be made in the air (volleyed).

    Typical **pickleball** games are played to eleven points (and must be won by a margin of two or more points). A key feature of the pickleball court is the 7' x 20' area immediately on both sides of the net, which is called the Non Volley Zone (NVZ). Players must remain outside this zone while hitting a volley (a ball that has not bounced) or on the follow-through step after a volley.

    Individual **pickleball** games are usually finished in about 15-20 minutes, and this allows other players to rotate onto the court(s) and provides rest for those who may be tired. All ages can play **pickleball**, but especially those persons between the ages of 15 and 85. You don't need to be an athlete to learn the game and have a good time!

    Basic **pickleball** paddles are available in Aitkin, MN via AHS Community Education, or the lighter composite paddles can be borrowed from an instructor during an introductory class, so that no one needs to invest immediately in their own equipment other than a pair of good quality (white-soled) court shoes. **Pickleball** *"addicts"* are encouraged to buy their own paddles, however.

Pickleball can be really fun to play under these conditions:
- You learn the rules and abide by them.
- You agree to play fair (engage in good sportsmanship).
- You acquire some skills and useful tactics through coaching and practice.
- You can laugh at yourself and others, and they can laugh at you.
- You know how to prevent injuries (i.e., by stretching in advance, or keeping yourself hydrated, or playing within your physical capacity). Your instructor will stress safety, but each player is responsible for his/her own health. In particular, *don't back up* in an attempt to return a deep ball! (Trust me.)

More information: Contact the author at 218-428-2439.

See also the USAPA website (and history of pickleball) at USAPA.org.

TRUTHS AND HALF-TRUTHS ABOUT PICKLEBALL

1. The origin of pickleball dates back to 1965.

2. The name of the game is derived from one* of the following sources:

   a. The centuries-old practice of roaming Vikings entertaining themselves during long voyages at sea by batting pickles (instead of a ball) back and forth from bow to stern with their oars.

   b. An occasion (cited in the annals of "strange events I have seen") occurred in which a victim of a purse-snatching, when faced with a police line-up of Bill, Tom, Les, and George immediately told the police sergeant, "*I pick Les.*"

   c. There was a moment when the field workers in a southern cotton plantation weighed their output at the end of the day and compared it against the employer's daily standard of 300 pounds. "I pick more," boasted Maria. "I pick exactly that much," exclaimed Francis. "*I pick les',*" said little Johnny.

   d. One summer day on Bainbridge Island, Washington Joel Pritchard's dog ("Pickles") would chase any errant ball during early versions of the game and then run away with it as though claiming it to be his own, thus producing the term "*Pickle's ball*" (pickleball).

3. The United States of America Pickleball Association (USAPA) reports that there are over 3 million pickleballers playing at over 6,000 courts. The sport continues to gain visibility through a variety of local, regional, and national tournaments and the efforts of 1,500 area "Ambassadors" (including J. Mortswen) who promote and facilitate the game.

4. The USAPA (formed in 1984) supports and encourages professionalism by participants through the development of an Official Rulebook, guidelines for player rating levels, and programs for standardizing pickleball instruction and the certification of referees.

5. All pickleballs and paddles used in sanctioned tournaments must have received prior approval by the USAPA. Homemade paddles are unacceptable. No paddles can be longer than 17" nor can the combined length and width exceed 24". However, there are no limits on either paddle thickness or paddle weight. Balls must weigh less than about 1 ounce and have a diameter less than about 3 inches.

6. Different balls are recommended for use in outdoor and indoor pickleball games. The outdoor ball has more holes (up to 40 smaller ones), while the indoor ball typically has less holes (26 or more) and larger ones. Pickleballs, originally white, now come in a rainbow of different colors (e.g., yellow, orange, lime, pink).

7. A wide variety of instructional materials and visual demonstrations of various aspects of pickleball are available on the Internet.

* "D" is the preferred answer to item 2.

WE LOVE PICKLEBALL BECAUSE...

1. It is relatively easy to learn (not a steep learning curve).

2. It has a funny name, but makes for a terrific game.

3. It provides great physical exercise at any level of play.

4. It satisfies our need for competition, achievement, and competence.

5. It is "knock your socks off" fun to play, and provides great opportunities for good-natured kidding and laughter.

6. It provides numerous health benefits. It lowers blood pressure, boosts immune systems, reduces stress, improves mental acuity, stimulates blood flow, aids weight loss, and improves joint flexibility.

7. It is relatively inexpensive to buy the equipment and to play on public courts.

8. It is played on a much smaller court than tennis, making it easier to cover the playing area.

9. It has a much simpler (and more logical) scoring system than tennis (with the latter's traditional ad, deuce, and love terms and 15-30-40 scoring).

10. As a "sport for life," it is enjoyed by people of all ages.

11. There are thousands of courts across the country, so it is easy to find places to play.

12. It has a great social aspect, where you can meet and develop new friendships each time you play.

13. It allows players to hit with power, touch, spin, and angles.

14. It lends itself to different strategies (soft and controlled, power and pace, stacking formations, etc.).

15. Rapid volley exchanges are commonplace and exciting.

16. It is a growth sport, with millions of players worldwide.

17. It has an official sanctioning body (USAPA) that sets the rules and provides a variety of supportive materials.

18. It is gender-neutral and age-neutral; anyone can play and become competent.

19. Once bitten by the "pickleball bug," it is addictive.

20. It keeps you young at heart!

BENEFICIAL EFFECTS OF PIC

The game of pickleball is one contemporary fc
that is enjoyed by millions of players. The purpc
are to refresh, entertain, divert attention, amuse, c
delight, gratify, please, relieve, renew, and reanim;
a nutshell, as the actors in the movie *The Bucket*
heaven's gatekeepers will ask prospective entrants two questions
(to which they had better have good answers):
    1. Did you find joy in *your* life?
    2. Did you bring joy to *others*?
Passionate pickleballers can most likely respond affirmatively to
both of those queries, thus almost assuring themselves of eternal
tranquility!

    Advocates of pickleball assert that the game is "fast,
exciting, a source of good physical and mental exercise, a chance
to laugh at oneself, an opportunity for stress relief, a vehicle for
having fun, a chance to make new friends and socialize with them,
and a delightful way to burn off some calories." It is all of that, and
even more, of course.

SPECIFIC BENEFITS

    Pickleball provides its players with a chance to learn and
grow and stretch their minds and bodies; it provides a pathway to
satisfaction of one's powerful needs for personal achievement and
competence; it tests one's resilience; it demands participants to be
in the present and focus on what is in front of them; it invites us to
laugh at our own foibles; it reduces feelings of loneliness and
isolation; it improves balance; it provides its players with a sense
of purpose; and it allows us to appreciate excellence in ourselves
and others.

BROADER PAYOFFS

    Among its broader benefits is the fact that playing
pickleball is a lifestyle change for many participants—one that
leads toward physical and mental fitness and enhances one's sense
of well-being rather than thinking only of one's ailments. The
social connections engendered through pickleball stimulate its

to get more sleep, eat healthier foods, attain peace of mind, lower their stress levels, while a sense of purpose leads to a reduced risk of mortality, stroke, heart attack, and Alzheimer's disease. It also contributes to getting more exercise and avoidance of drug abuse and alcohol addiction.

EXERCISE IS BENEFICIAL

The National Center for Health Statistics (of the CDC) reports that less than one-quarter of U.S. adults meet the recommended guidelines for both aerobic and muscle-strengthening exercise. The good news is that when older adults *do* exercise regularly (such as by playing pickleball several times weekly), scientific studies show that they:

1. Have far less loss of brain functioning,
2. Have less brain blood vessel damage,
3. Have improved memory,
4. Have better spatial memory,
5. Have a greater ability to learn new facts,
6. Are better able to handle Parkinson's disease,
7. Have a lower risk of falls in the home,
8. Can help stave off the natural effects of dementia, and
9. Are 56% less likely to die of cardiovascular diseases.

In conclusion, although most recreational pickleballers play for fun, there is an amazingly wide array of positive side effects as well. In contrast to the cynical admonition to "pick one's poison" from among a set of troublesome consequences, pickleballers can enjoy one or all of the documented side benefits described above. Enjoy the journey, and extend your life in good health!

PURCHASING A PICKLEBALL PADDLE

You may possibly be considering the purchase of a pickleball paddle of your own. Wooden paddles are often used in high school physical education programs, as their primary advantages are low cost and longer durability under sometimes-careless conditions of use. In general, however, I don't favor them for regular adult usage. Instead, there are several factors to consider in making a paddle purchase.

Weight is a primary factor in purchasing a new paddle. In general, lighter paddles (e.g., 7 ounces) can move at a greater speed and are easier to manipulate on the court. However, they may not exhibit enough force to assist a player when serving, returning a serve, making a lob, or slamming the ball for a put-away shot. Heavier paddles (e.g., 8 ounces) provide more impact at the time of contact with the ball, but may also slow down your paddle speed and put a greater strain on the player's wrist, arm, and shoulder.

Lightweight paddles can weigh as little as 6 ounces, with very heavy paddles weighing over 10 ounces. It is surprising how much differently just a few more (or less) ounces of paddle weight can feel. Most commercially available paddles for beginner and intermediate players weigh between 7 and 9 ounces.

Grip size is equally important, as hand size (finger length) varies substantially among players. Most grips are 4 to 4.5 inches in circumference. Holding a paddle in the most common grip, there should ideally remain a small space between your finger tips and the palm of your hand.

Although paddles come in somewhat different shapes (rectangular to nearly oval to round), I feel their **composition** (e.g., graphite or aluminum or fiberglass), color, and decorative designs are far less important to recreational players than weight in choosing a paddle.

I spent about two weeks one summer trying out various paddles and talking to a small group of friends for their advice (who seldom agreed) before I bought my newest paddle (an Engage "Poach" model with a fairly light weight since I feel that I am capable of providing the arm strength and hand speed necessary to provide the "pop" that I desire on put-away shots). I also think that a lighter weight paddle gives me more "feel" for the pickleball on dink shots at the NVZ line.

Paddle **noise** can even be a factor in paddle selection. For example, if you plan to play pickleball in your backyard or driveway, your neighbors might appreciate your ownership of quieter paddles that have a less-distinctive "pop" when you hit the ball.

Cost is also a factor when committing to a recreational sport. Most pickleball paddles range in price between about $40 and $150, with many good ones available for about $60-$80. (More expensive is not necessarily better for most social players.) In addition, some retailers and on-line sellers will periodically sell slightly used "demo" paddles at significant discounts.

To me, the most important factor in a purchase is simply the *"feel"* you get with each one. Does it give you confidence? Can you swing it with authority throughout an extended game or playing session without getting tired? Can you grip it comfortably? Some on-line paddle sellers will let you experiment with a paddle for 30 days before finalizing your purchase. See, for example, www.pickleballcentral.com.

Ideally, you should only buy a USAPA-approved paddle that has been tested for conformity to their specifications, in case you ever play in a sanctioned tournament.

KEY PICKLEBALL TERMS & THEIR DEFINITIONS

(Source: Adapted from the USAPA/IFP Official Rulebook)

BODY SHOT—Being hit in any part of the body (often the torso) by an opponent's shot.

CARRY—Hitting the ball so that it slides across the face of the paddle during its forward motion. (This is *legal*, if the motion is continuous.)

DINK SHOT—A soft and low shot that arcs over the net and lands in the NVZ.

DOUBLE BOUNCE—Any ball that bounces more than once on one side of the net. This is a fault.

DROP SHOT—A groundstroke that falls short of the opponent's position, making it difficult to return.

FAULT—Any action that stops play because of a rule violation or interference.

GET—A successful return of a shot that was difficult to reach ("get to it").

GROUNDSTROKE—Hitting the ball from anywhere after one bounce.

HINDER—Any element or occurrence that negatively affects play (e.g., a stray ball, non-playing person, or object near the court or overhead).

LET—A serve that hits the net cord and lands in the service court. (A let serve will be replayed).

LOB—A shot that returns the ball high and deep to the opponent's court.

NO MAN'S LAND—The unofficial designation of the middle third (front to back) of the area between the non-volley zone and the baseline; an area on which players should minimize their time because of the probability of opponent shots landing at their feet.

NON VOLLEY ZONE (NVZ)—The 7-foot-deep section of the court adjacent to and on both sides of the net (including all lines defining the zone) in which you may not *volley* the ball.

OVERHEAD SMASH—A hard, overhead shot usually resulting from an opponent's lob, high return, or very high bounce.

PASSING SHOT—A shot designed to prevent the opponent's return of the ball by placing a line drive (or soft shot) close to the sideline (out of the opponent's reach).

POACHING—The act of suddenly intercepting a shot from one's opponent by reaching or moving laterally and crossing the mid-court line.

RALLY—Continuous play that occurs after the serve and before a fault.

REPLAYS—Any rallies that are played again for any reason without the awarding of a point or a side out.

SECOND SERVE—The special condition when the designated team first begins a game (or when a team loses the first of its two allocated service opportunities).

SERVE—Striking the ball in the air in an underhand motion at the beginning of a service opportunity so as to land in the opponent's crosscourt service court while clearing the net and the NVZ line.

SERVICE COURT—The area on either side of the centerline bounded by the NVZ line, the baseline, and the sideline. All lines are included (valid) in the service court on the receipt of serve *except the NVZ line.*

SHADOWING—The act of moving in concert with one's partner so as to synchronize their movements and play as an integrated team.

SIDE OUT—When one side or team loses its (two) service opportunities in a sequence and the other side is awarded the opportunity to serve.

UNFORCED ERRORS—Mistakes made by players that were the result of miss-hits or carelessness, and not simply caused by quality shots from their opponents.

VOLLEY—Hitting the ball in the air during a rally before the ball has a chance to bounce on the court. (This is legal *after* the return of serve and if made from behind the NVZ line.)

WHY DO I EMPHASIZE THE NEED TO KNOW PB RULES?

On the next page ("Rules, Rules, and More Rules") I have laid out some of the more fundamental concepts from the USAPA Rulebook. In my introductory sessions on pickleball, I invariably emphasize the importance of all players knowing these rules (as well as how to play safely and courteously). New players should, however, question an instructor as to *why* time is spent on the rules and not just embrace them blindly. I fully recognize that rule books are often detailed and boring to read/study, but it is highly likely that at some point in one's playing career an argument can be avoided if all participants have familiarized themselves with the essential rules.

There are numerous compelling reasons to *learn* the rules of pickleball, as well as to *follow* them. I will delineate several of them.

Individual Competence. It is satisfying (and enjoyable) to play with confidence. A major contributing factor to confidence lies in overall competence. Part of this competence lies in an understanding of the overall game and its underlying rules. *Anyone*, regardless of skill level, can (and should) gain comprehension of the rulebook. (How could anyone claim that they are fully competent if they don't first grasp and retain knowledge about the foundational rules of the sport in question?)

Individual Completeness. Good players don't simply rely on their skills, strategies, athleticism, and mental agility. To become complete players, they also know the USAPA rulebook from cover to cover so that they will know what they can and cannot (legally) do on the court. At almost any level of player competence (ratings), situations arise that require reference to the rules and interpretation thereof. Without this knowledge, they can potentially be at a disadvantage.

Interpersonal Structure. Although I have often been called upon (as a local 'expert" to identify and explain a rule situation), it is much more useful when *multiple* players are familiar with the rules (i.e., in case of one person's absence, or an unclear interpretation). This allows for convergence of explanations, and thus increases the validity and acceptance of the rule within the group of players.

Transferability. When players visit different courts in various parts of the country (such as when "northerners" migrate to southern climes during the winter), it is possible that they will encounter "local" (or even "loose") interpretations of the rules. It is helpful to be able to speak with authority (almost quoting "chapter and verse") in these situations.

Competitive Advantage. A final argument for learning the rules is that, just like in major sports such as football, basketball, golf, or baseball, there may occur moments when the ability to invoke a rule can work in your favor. It would be tragic *not* to be able to use a rule to your advantage in those situations.

Conclusion: The USAPA/IFP Rulebook is small in size (5" x 8.5"), relatively short (46 pages prior to a section on tournaments and referees), visually spaced between lines, and clearly written. Readable within an hour, there is little reason *not* to become knowledgeable about the rules of pickleball!

RULES, RULES, AND MORE RULES

Here are some of the basic pickleball rules that beginners should be aware of:

1. The game of pickleball is usually played to 11 points, and must be won with a two-point margin. Only the *serving* team can score points. Each of the team's two servers (in a doubles game) gets only one fault (*team* error) during a series before the opportunity to serve goes to the opponents.

2. The serve *must* be made *underhand* with the paddle in an upward motion, striking the ball while it is below the waist (one's navel). The serve *must* land in the diagonally opposite rectangle bounded by the baseline, sideline, centerline, and non-volley zone line before the opponent may hit it. After each successful serve (and point), the server moves to the alternate side of his/her court and serves again. As a special note, at the beginning of a game, the team that has the ball first only gets to have *one* player serve; after a single team fault, the other team serves and thereafter each team gets two faults per series.

3. After the receiving team returns the serve, the serving team *must* also let the ball bounce (the **"two-bounce rule"**) before hitting it. After that, either team is allowed to strike the ball in the air (a 'volley').

4. When a new *series* begins (after two faults by the opponents), the player standing on his/her right-hand side of the court becomes 'Server #1' in *that* new series. This numerical assignment is independent of who was "Server #1" in any previous series.

5. Any ball that hits the baseline or sideline during play is 'good;' pickleball etiquette always gives the benefit of the doubt to the *opposing* team. On the serve, a ball hitting the non-volley zone (NVZ) line is NOT good; it is a fault.

6. A unique feature of pickleball is the existence of the *NVZ* (an area 7' deep x 20' wide on both sides of the net). *This is a safety zone*, wherein a player may not stand (or step into on the follow through) when hitting a volleyed ball. However, any player *may* enter the NVZ at any time to

return a ball that has bounced *within* it. Any player (including oneself or partner or opponent) may call a fault at the NVZ line. Players who step on the NVZ line (or into the zone) during or immediately after a volley initiated by them is guilty of a fault, and *must* call it on themselves.

7. The scoring in pickleball can be confusing at first but is really quite simple. Before serving, a player *must* clearly announce the three parts of the score in this order:

   a. The current serving team's score;

   b. The current receiving team's score;

   c. Identification of the server # (e.g., '1' or '2') in *this* series.

   For example, the second server of a serving team that is behind by 4 points might say "5-9-2." If this team faults, the opponents would then get the ball and the first server (in the right hand corner) announces the score as "9-5-1."

8. At the start of a serve, player positions are as follows:

   a. The server *must* be behind the baseline, & between the center & sideline.

   b. The server's partner is *advised* to be behind the baseline, so as to be prepared for the return of serve (the 'two-bounce' rule).

   c. The returner *should* be positioned on or behind his/her baseline to best be prepared for a deep serve (or to move forward for a short serve).

   d. The returner's partner *should* be positioned immediately behind the NVZ on his/her side of the centerline. This is an advantageous location!

Note that only the server is bound by the rules regarding where to stand; the other three players have more flexibility in their choice of position.

BASIC PICKLEBALL SUGGESTIONS

1. Wear sunscreen—and wide-brimmed hats—every time.
   (Why? You DON'T want skin cancer.)

2. Warm up and stretch before playing.
   (Why? You DON'T want to pull a muscle.)

3. Drink plenty of liquid—before, during, and after play.
   (Why? You DON'T want to get dehydrated & faint. Liquid also helps you to avoid leg cramps.)

4. Don't engage in unsafe behaviors (e.g., running forward and losing your balance, running backward [backpedaling]).
   (Why? You DON'T want to risk serious injury to yourself.)

5. Obtain good equipment—your shoes, your paddle, etc.
   (Why? You want to be comfortable, safe, and familiar with your playing equipment.)

6. Learn the rules of pickleball, as well as the strategies.
   (Why? It would be chaos without rules, and good strategies help you and your partner improve the quality of your play.)

7. Demonstrate your etiquette and courtesy at all times (in standing, walking, line calls, ball returns, scoring, personal language, and fault calls).
   (Why? You don't want a bad reputation, do you?)

8. Resolve to practice your skills and focus on improving one element of your game each time you play; ask for advice/guidance from instructors and coaches.
   (Why? You DO want to get better, don't you?)

9. Be a team player by communicating with your partner, helping him/her be in the correct position, praising his/her success, and taking appropriate responsibility for problems and your own errors.
   (Why? "There is no *'I'* in 'team'.")

10. Be sure to alert players on other courts if a ball goes astray by yelling "Ball on Court!" as loudly and repeatedly as necessary until you have everyone's attention.

(Why? You DON'T want to be responsible for serious injury to anyone else, do you?)

11. **Have fun!** (Relax; joke around; don't be afraid to look silly or awkward; get to know your fellow pickleballers, for they are almost universally nice people.)

(Why? Why ELSE would you play except to **have fun**?)

SAFETY, ETIQUETTE, & ETHICS

I have always vowed that if I prepared a book on pickleball, the topic of safety would appear early and not be inserted toward the end. It is *vitally* important, and needs to be stressed repeatedly. Here are some guidelines to follow on three different topics.

SAFETY:
1. Wear proper shoes with laces tied firmly. (Do NOT play in sandals or bare feet.)
2. Stretch your legs, feet, arms, and back in advance of playing to loosen up various muscles and joints.
3. Drink plenty of liquids before, during, and after playing.
4. Apply liberal amounts of sunscreen.
5. Move backwards and forwards with extreme caution (if done at all) to avoid falling.
6. Don't walk closely behind a court (until play stops between points) to avoid being hit by a player's paddle on the backswing.
7. Loudly yell "Ball on Court" to alert players on adjacent courts about stepping on stray balls.
8. *Never* play on a wet (outdoor) court.
9. Remove foreign objects (leaves, twigs, sand) from the outdoor court to avoid slipping.
10. Compete within your *own* capabilities; don't try for 'miracle' shots.
11. Strongly consider wearing protective glasses.
12. Communicate with your partners to avoid running into each other or hitting them with your paddle.
13. If you should lose your balance and fall, try to 'hit and roll' rather than bracing yourself with your outstretched arms. Keep your head up if you fall backwards so as to avoid a concussion!
14. Pick up and secure loose pickleballs to avoid having them roll onto the court when the wind blows.

ETIQUETTE:

1. Do not walk behind players when an active point is being played, for this is a distraction to them.
2. If you are not ready to begin play of a new point, hold your paddle up in the air (or your extended arm), or turn your back on the opponent.
3. When serving, call the score and then pause before serving so as to avoid catching the receiver off guard.
4. Call the score loudly enough so the *opponent* can clearly hear it.
5. On sunny or windy days, agree in advance to switch sides when the first team reaches a score of "6."
6. Control your temper (and your language).
7. After a point is over, return the ball politely and safely to your opponent. NEVER slam the ball at the other side of the court.
8. Greet your opponents before a game and introduce yourself; meet them after a game to congratulate (e.g., touching paddles) and thank them for playing

ETHICS AND SPORTSMANSHIP:

1. Make line calls fairly. Err on the side of your opponent.
2. Do not make line calls on the opponent's side of the court unless asked.
3. Call foot faults on yourself or your partner at the NVZ line. Note that you can also call foot faults at the NVZ line on your opponents.
4. If your partner calls a ball "out" but you believe it to be "in," speak up and agree to call it "in."
5. Never engage in distracting behavior (excess noise; distracting movement). See Rule 11.J.

FALLING: PREVENTION TRUMPS REACTION

People over 60 years old are often warned of the dangers of falling in (or outside) their homes. Slipping on smooth (or wet or icy) surfaces, tripping on rugs, falling in bathtubs, or running into unseen objects are just a few of the ways in which injuries occur in that setting. As one wag put it, "the world is full of banana peels."

Participation in active physical endeavors such as pickleball also puts players at risk of falling. Sometimes the only result is a skinned knee or wounded pride, but more serious products include sprains, cuts, broken bones, crushed vertebrae, and traumatic brain injuries. In addition, each fall can plant a seed of fearing future falls, and that can become a self-fulfilling prophecy. Wise players take a two-pronged approach to this issue—prevention and reaction (treatment).

Preventing falls on the pickleball court is highly preferred. Strategies for prevention include:
1. Having your eyesight checked regularly,
2. Refusing to play on a wet court (or one covered with any foreign objects),
3. Practicing mindfulness (not being distracted by other thoughts),
4. Having shoes that properly fit you and are not worn out,
5. Maintaining your balance,
6. Not backing up to hit a lobbed ball,
7. Being aware of possible obstacles and hazards (i.e., fence proximity, chairs, paddles, or balls) in the area,
8. Maintaining proper liquid intake so as to avoid dehydration,
9. Playing within your capabilities (not attempting a miracle shot),
10. Communicating with your partner so that you don't collide with each other.

Reacting well is important, too. Once you feel that a fall is imminent, here (from *AARP Magazine*) is a 5-step plan for *reacting* to a fall and making a safer crash landing:

1. *Stay bent* (flexible) with your elbows and knees. Avoid a FOOSH (Falling On Out Stretched Hands), which often results in a broken wrist or cracked elbow.
2. *Protect your head.* If you are falling forward, turn your face to one side; if falling backward, tuck your head toward your chest.
3. *Land on your meat.* Try to land on the fleshier portion of your anatomy so as to protect your elbows, knees, tailbone, and hips.
4. *Keep your body moving.* Fight the instinct to stop the fall quickly, but give in to the fall and roll to spread the impact across a larger part of your body.
5. *Finally, acknowledge and accept the fact that you fell.* Too many PB players immediately say "I'm OK" and try to get back on their feet. Stay on the ground and let bystanders tend to you; drink some liquids; rest on a bench; inventory your body for unfelt injuries. Know that some effects of a fall (such as a hematoma) may show up hours or even days later. Seek medical care if in doubt.

PROPER HYDRATION FOR PICKLEBALLERS*

The voice of Mario Lanza, in the movie adaptation of Sigmund Romberg's *The Student Prince*, beseeched the group assembled in the bar to "Drink, Drink, Drink..." Although the objective of that song might be morally questionable to some, we can easily adapt the message to suggest the adequate intake of water or similar liquids as a means to prevent dehydration during pickleball games.

What is proper hydration? Normally, you should ingest about 64 ounces of liquid per day. *More* is required on hot days or those days with increased physical activity, whether it occurs at work or during play. Note that in some tournament formats, players may be required to play multiple games in a round-robin format, or play successive sets of games (2 out of 3) for several hours as they work their way up the ladder to a championship match.

When to do it? Simply put, drink *substantial* amounts of liquids before, during, and after exercise. Don't wait until you feel symptoms (i.e., dizziness) arising!

Why do it? Several powerful rationales exist for hydration; most typically you want to avoid fatigue, muscle cramps, dizziness, or fainting. Drinking liquids helps to regulate your body's temperature, lubricate your joints, and maintain peak performance. Every cell in every organ in your body (e.g., muscles, heart, brain) requires constant hydration.

Failure to properly hydrate can result in dry mouth, lightheadedness, nausea, vomiting, sweating, rapid breathing, increased heart rate, low blood pressure, confusion, muscle spasms or cramps, weakness, cold hands and feet, fatigue, or loss of coordination. Any of these require immediate attention. Inform your partner or a bystander if you experience any of these symptoms.

How to do it? Drink water, fruit juices, or Gatorade-type products. Alternatively, eat fruits and vegetables high in liquid content (such as cucumbers, tomatoes, watermelon, bell peppers, grapes, cantaloupe, oranges, apples, or blueberries).

*Adapted from/expanded on a similar article by Jeff Shank, Tipbit #207.

CHAPTER 2

Getting Started: Serves, Returns, & Line Calls

THE SERVE, PART 1

According to some players and coaches, the serve is the *most important shot* in pickleball. Why? This is simply because *if the ball is not put into play, then your team can never score.* If your team never scores, then the only thing your opponents need to win is to have a *pulse*! Furthermore, if one partner cannot serve adequately, the other partner will soon become frustrated. *Both* players need a certain level of competency.

Legal serves: What are they?   According to the USAPA rulebook, there are several standards for servers to be aware of, as follows:

1.   The server must stand behind the baseline and between the imaginary extensions of the sideline and the centerline in order to avoid a foot fault.

2.   Contact of the paddle with a ball must be made below your waist (e.g., your navel).

3.   The paddle must be traveling in an upward arc (not sidearm or overhead).

4.   The paddle head must be below the wrist joint when the ball is struck.

5.   The ball must be struck before the ball hits the ground; it cannot be bounced and then (immediately) hit.

6.   Following contact, the ball must clear the net and land in the opponent's court (*beyond* the NVZ line). Note that if the served ball touches the net and lands in the receiver' court beyond the non volley zone line, it is a "let" and will be replayed. However, if it touches the net and falls elsewhere, it is a fault.

The mechanics and strategies of a good serve:

1. Use an underhand motion such as that used in bowling, softball pitching, or horseshoe throwing.

2.   Angle your non-paddle shoulder toward your target to allow a clean swing
across your torso.

3.   Point your left toe for right-handers) forward toward your target.

4. Begin by swinging your paddle to the rear until it is parallel with the ground.

4. Place (drop at the last instant) the ball into your forward-moving paddle, while keeping your eyes on the ball.

5. Bend your knees and contact the ball when it is low to the ground.

6. Step toward your target with the front foot (the left foot for right-handed players) to add bodily momentum to the ball.

7. Follow through with your paddle in the direction of your target after you make contact.

8. Swing *through* the ball with energy; don't simply strike *at* it.

9. Have a specific target area in mind for your serve.

10. Stay back (or step back) behind the baseline to prepare for your opponent's deep return.

11. Set a (high) goal for your success rate; monitor your success.

12. In the beginning of your learning curve, aim for the middle of the opponent's court so as to minimize errors. Remember that a good serve is one that falls correctly into the opponent's court and initiates a rally.

13. As you gain confidence and accuracy, consider:

a. trying for deep serves;

b. varying the pace;

c. aiming for the opponent's backhand side;

d. using an occasional lob serve.

THE SERVE, PART 2

Faults. In pickleball, a *fault* is any violation of the rules that results in a stoppage of play. There are several examples of *service* faults that may occur:
- If the server swings and misses the ball;
- If a served ball strikes any object (e.g., the net, or the net post);
- If the served ball touches the server's partner or oneself;
- If the served ball lands *on* the opponent's NVZ line;
- If the served ball lands *before* the opponent's NVZ line;
- If the served ball lands *outside* the opponent's service court;
- If the served ball hits the net and misses the opponent's service court;
- If the wrong player makes the serve;
- If the server uses an illegal serving motion;
- If the server serves from the wrong court.

Replays. In general, there are relatively few reasons for players to replay a point (unless it occurs within an introductory training session and the instructor simply wants a new player to achieve some success before moving on). However, service "lets" represent legitimate reasons to replay a point, such as when:
- The serve touches the net and is otherwise good (i.e., it falls into the appropriate space on the receiver's court);
- The receiver appropriately signaled "not ready" *before* the serve motion was initiated;
- The serve touches the net and hits an opponent;
- "Ball on court" is called during the service;
- Interference by a spectator or another court's player occurs.
- Note: there is no limit to the number of service lets allowed.

Targets. Service strategies (possible target areas) include:
- Deep to the receiver's forehand side (near the far corner);
- Deep to the receiver's feet;

- Deep to the receiver's backhand side;
- Short (near the NVZ line but in the service court);
- High (lob serve that is sometimes difficult for a receiver to return with any pace on it).

Special notes:
- The player's hand (*below* the wrist) is considered to be part of the paddle any time during a rally.
- Any ball in play that strikes a permanent object (e.g., ceiling, or basketball hoop) before the ball touches the floor is a fault by the hitting team.
- The serving team must let the ball bounce on their side before striking the return of serve (a groundstroke) so as not to violate the "Double Bounce Rule."
- Any serve that first touches the receiver or the receiver's partner is a point for the serving team.
- The serve can easily be practiced on your own to gain proficiency. Do so!
- The service motion can be practiced anywhere— preferably in front of a mirror or observer who can provide feedback to the server.

THE "LOWDOWN" ON POSTURE*

Body Down and "Paddle up!" Both your stance and your ready position are important at the beginning of each point and *throughout* each (and every) point. This means you don't do it sometimes; you learn to do it all the time.

It begins with the position in which you hold your paddle just prior to the beginning of each point (unless you are the server). Hold the paddle (using the appropriate grip) in front of your chest so that you can literally "see" the paddle while looking ahead. This not only prepares you for the next shot, but also helps you keep your balance as a counterweight to your body. In addition, always having your *"paddle up"* is an important signal to your partner that you are mentally and physically ready to play; it also serves as a reminder for your teammate to do the same.

What should you do about your posture? Keep your entire body down (low), as opposed to standing straight up (erect). This is my admonition to myself (a naturally stiff-postured Scandinavian) to "Bend your knees!"

Why do this? The benefits from staying low start with the mere fact that your head (and eyes) will then be closer to the path or flight of the oncoming ball. This gives you a better perspective of the ball's trajectory and spin, so you'll be able to see (and track) it better as it comes toward you. Further, and more importantly, it keeps your body (torso) more in line with the ball, limiting the amount you need to move down to the ball from shot to shot (because you're already there). This crouched (bent knee) position readies and allows you to move more quickly than if you were standing erect. Being low and staying low helps your stroke mechanics, too. Essentially, you always want to keep your body movement close to the ground. Finally, *this position will help you feel and be more engaged in each point!*

How to do this? Getting down low starts at the knees. This means you must bend (flex) your knees considerably. Picture yourself as about to sit down in a chair, but lean forward a bit so that you don't begin to tip backwards and lose your balance. Here is a good mental image: picture yourself as a crouched panther about to pounce on your prey. Your focus is forward looking and your eyes are attentively following the path of your opponent's paddle and the subsequent flight of the ball toward you.

Practice. Try a little practice of this technique the next chance you get (maybe simply in your warm-up before play). Initially, hit some soft dinks at the NVZ, getting low by bending your knees to help you "lift" the ball. Then stay low the whole time. Next, try a volley/volley exchange, again getting and staying low. Now move back to the baseline and exchange groundstrokes. *You'll immediately discover how much better you can see and react to the ball,* because your eyes are on the same plane as the ball.

Visual reminder. One pickleball clinic instructor gave me this rather "earthy" image to use: he said simply (and poetically) "A** to the grass!" Note that this prescription also applies vividly to the ideal groundstroke when you hit a rising ball just after it has made contact with the court. *You need to be low!*

Repeat this mantra to yourself..."Get down low, stay down low, but hold your paddle up high." It works, so try it!

*Adapted from material distributed by Jeff Shank.

RECEIVING THE SERVE; MOVING UP

What should the receiver of the serve know and do?
1. The receiver is the player diagonally across from the server.
2. The receiver is responsible to be ready once the server calls the score.
3. The receiver should check one's partner to be sure s/he is ready.
4. The receiver is the only person who may return (touch) a served ball.
5. The receiver's partner may stand anywhere on or off the court.
6. If the wrong partner acts as the receiver, it is a fault.
7. Either the receiver or his/her partner may (and should) make "Let" or "Out" calls instantly.
8. The receiver may signal "not ready" before the serve by:
   • Visibly holding up one's paddle.
   • Visibly holding up one's arm.
   • Turning your back on the server.
9. The receiving team faults if:
   • Receiver fails to hit the ball.
   • Receiver fails to return the ball over net.
   • Receiver hits the ball out of bounds.
   • Wrong player hits the return of serve.
   • Receiver touches the ball in midair (before it bounces).
   • Partner touches (or is touched by) the served ball in the air.
   • Either partner creates a substantial visual distraction or oral disturbance.
10. Returning team should have these primary objectives:
    • Keep the serving team pinned deep.
    • Join your partner at the NVZ line.
    • Attain better control of the future shot exchanges.
11. Advice to receivers:
    • Observe the server's prior tendencies (speed; direction; spin).
    • Bend (flex) your knees to keep your eyes low.

- Hold your "Paddle up" in the ready position (be prepared).
- Start watching the ball as soon as possible.
- Follow the ball's flight right into your paddle (don't look ahead).
- Position yourself so as to take most serves with your forehand.
- Practice backhand returns of serve so you are equally adept at using both return shots.
- Mix up your returns (low and firm; high and soft; short).
- Aim for a specific area (server's backhand or feet; middle of the court).

What should the receiver do *after* returning the serve?
- Instantly **move up** until your feet are just behind the NVZ line (a strategically strong place) by:
- Hitting high and deep returns.
- Using your shot momentum to *pull* you forwards.
- Taking quick strides or using "split steps" to progress to the NVZ line in stages.
- *Committing* to move up.
- Practicing it *every time* you receive a serve.

Why **should the receiver move up after striking the ball?** Because:
- Almost *every* good PB player rated 3.5, 4.0, or 4.5 and above does so.
- It gives you more angled shots to make when you are closer to the NVZ line.
- It allows you to return opponents' groundstrokes quicker.
- It allows you to catch opponents off guard with your drop shots.
- It puts you in great position to hit smashes.
- It's a lot more FUN when you are in position to hit volleys!

GUIDELINES FOR THE FOREHAND OR BACKHAND STROKE

The **forehand** and **backhand** strokes are used primarily for low, flat shots made at your baseline, beginning with the return of serve. However, they are also used in longer rallies from that area, and serve as the foundation for a defensive lob or the third shot drop. The two basic strokes are, in effect, basically mirror images of each other.

The forehand stroke begins with the player moving his/her feet to get in position. The backswing moves the paddle into a low position such that the shot will have a moderate upward motion to it sufficient to drive the ball forward and over the net. Both the leading foot and the left shoulder (for a right-hander) should be pointed toward the target. The forward motion is largely accomplished through movement of the torso and an arm hinged at the shoulder. The paddle should end up pointed high and toward (or past) your target.

Here are some suggestions:

1. Always begin at the "ready" position (feet spread somewhat apart, and paddle up and in front of you) so that you are ready to move to the ball.
2. Flex your knees (so you aren't stiff).
3. Watch the ball from the moment it strikes your opponent's paddle (to see where it is coming to you).
4. Move your feet (slide or shuffle sideways, if necessary) so that you will have sufficient room between the ball and your body to make a free arm swing at the ball.
5. Start pushing/pulling your paddle back with your non-dominant hand (to help you make a complete shoulder turn, and to coil up your strength). Your non-dominant shoulder and arm should now point at your target.
6. Keep your eyes on the ball until it strikes your own paddle. Make a small oral sound at the moment it hits your paddle (to remind you to be attentive).
7. Step across your body and forward with your left foot (for right-handers).

8. You should plan to contact the ball when it is still in front of you (approximately even with your front foot).
9. Bend your knees so that you are under the ball when you strike it. Tilt your paddle slightly upward.
10. Step into the shot so that you are transferring your weight forward as you swing.
11. Imagine that you are hitting 3 or 4 consecutive pickleballs. Do this by keeping your paddle square (perpendicular) to your target at the point of contact and immediately thereafter. Do not make an "open gate" (tightly hinged) swing.
12. Make a full (high) finish to your swing, with the paddle winding up pointing to your opponent. (Don't strike *at* the ball; swing *through* the ball.)
13. Immediately return to the "ready" position to prepare for the next shot, or to move aggressively toward the NVZ line.

For a backhand stroke, the same process is used except that the right-handed player will step across with his/her right foot while swinging the paddle back behind the left side. Note that both of these two strokes can (and should) be practiced at home—preferably in front of a full-length mirror—so that they will be almost automatic during a game.

MAKING LINE CALLS

Rules are important in every sport, but common sense, etiquette, and courtesy are also critical elements in pickleball. We compete hard on the pickleball (PB) court, but in addition we need to be seen by others as fair in our judgments so that we all have fun (and maybe even like each other!). Arguments shouldn't be necessary, and should be avoided.

What are the national *rules* that govern line calls? As you might expect, the answer is not always simple, but I will draw heavily from (and quote parts of) Section 6 of the 64-page 2018 USAPA Rule book (which governs tournament play in pickleball).

First, let's clarify **which team** can make the call. The answer here is very clear and unambiguous—*Players can ONLY call the lines (sidelines and baseline) on their side of the court (net)*. The other team should NOT offer their opinion (unless it is asked of them), as they usually are NOT in a very good position to see the ball clearly when it is 20-40 feet away from them. (Similarly, *spectators* on the sidelines should not be consulted on line calls (nor should they offer their opinion). To sum up: *only the two members of the receiving team should make line calls*; they should strive for accuracy; and the opponents should *not* question the line calls made. To adapt what President Jimmy Carter famously said many years ago ("Trust me"), we need to trust our opponents (and they need to be trustworthy).

Second, **when** should line calls be made? The answer is remarkably simple; it is *"instantly."* In action, this means that line calls should be made *before* the opponents hit the next shot. It also means that you and your partner don't have a "discussion" to determine the call; you make it loud and clear (or at least use hand signals pointing up [out] or down [in]) immediately.

Third, **who** makes the call? *Either* partner on a doubles team can do so, but preferably the person who is in the best *position* to see the ball. (This is often, but not always, the person who is closest to the line.)

Fourth, what if you **disagree** with your partner? The answer is straightforward—"If in doubt or disagreement, the ball must be declared *in*" (i.e., favoring your opponent). Furthermore, if the ball was not clearly seen by either partner, you should not immediately request to use a replay. However, you *may* ask the opposing team if they saw the ball and then if so, you must accept their ruling. In *friendly* games, opponents can assist by making an "out" call on their own shots, but should not argue for an "in" call favoring themselves.

Fifth, how about **close calls**? The rules state "a ball contacting the playing surface outside of the baseline or sideline, even though the edge of the ball overlaps the line, is considered *out of bounds.*"

Finally **what if a player yells "Out" or "No" or "Bounce it"** while the ball is *in the air*? This is deemed to be *player communication* and hence if the ball still lands "in" then *play will continue*. If the "out" call is made *after* the ball hits the playing surface outside of the sidelines or baseline, then it is deemed to be a line call and *play must stop (*even if a player has struck the ball).

Line calls are not always easy to make due to the speed of play and the presence of barriers to vision (i.e., the net or the partner's body). Above all, we should strive to demonstrate good sportsmanship through consistently fair line calls!

INDOOR vs. OUTDOOR PICKLEBALL COURTS*

In many parts of the country it is impractical to play outdoors all year long because of severe weather conditions (cold, snow, or ice in northern climes; heat, rain, and humidity in some southern climes). Pickleball players who wish to play all year long must then adapt to a variety of court venues (i.e., indoors in gymnasiums or private health clubs, or outdoors). As a result, a player may experience a concrete or tarred area at one time (outdoors), and a wooden or artificial court surface (indoors) at another time.

There are two primary **similarities** between the two types of sites, as follows:

• COURT SIZE--indoor and outdoor courts are identical in their dimensions.

• RULES—the rules are identical for both indoor and outdoor play.

The (much broader) **differences** (alphabetically) are these:

• AVAILABILITY. There are generally many more outdoor courts available and these courts tend to be available for greater periods of time.

• BACKGROUND. Walls and backgrounds in indoor courts often make it more difficult to see the ball and can even be different from one side to the other.

• BALL. The ball used indoors is quite different from the outdoor ball both in its playing characteristics and its overall appearance (i.e., lesser number of holes).

• HEIGHT. The height of the indoor court ceilings may be restrictive but, at the least, are considerably lower than outdoor courts where "the sky is the limit."

• INSECTS. Outdoor play can be affected adversely by pesky bugs such as flies, mosquitoes, gnats, bees, and ladybugs or beetles.

• LIGHTING. Indoor play may have dimmer lighting that causes visibility issues due to the positioning of the lights but at least they are not as blinding as that of the sun.

• NETS. Indoor nets are generally weaker and therefore clearly inferior (less predictable) to outdoor permanent nets.

• NOISE. The volume of indoor noise levels and the resulting echoes can become distracting to those players who prefer to concentrate.

• PRACTICE OPTIONS. Little or no time is available indoors versus almost limitless time outdoors for practice.

• PRICE. Indoor time usually charges an hourly or monthly fee to participants & outdoor courts are usually free.

• SPACING. Indoor courts are generally constructed in tighter quarters, and the spacing between courts is often compromised.

• SURFACE. Indoor court surfaces vary significantly from site to site while outdoor courts are generally quite similar from one to the next.

• WEATHER. Indoor courts control most weather issues (in particular, rain, snow, wind, cold, heat, and humidity) while outdoor courts are very limited in their capacity to do so (other than through the use of windscreens).

*Much of this analysis is drawn from a document by Jeff Shank.

CHAPTER 3

Essential Shots in Your Arsenal

THE PICKLEBALL VOLLEY*

What is a volley?
It is a shot made by hitting the ball *in the air* during a rally before the ball has a chance to bounce on your side of the court. (Volley shots are most often made while a player is at or near the NVZ line.)

Why do you hit a volley?
Volleys can be *offensive* in nature (as you attempt to win the point by hitting the ball hard, or downward, or well-placed toward the "golden middle," or any open space) or they can be *defensive* (saving a likely point when forced to hit the ball upward because it is below the height of the net). When a successful volley is made, it is informally called a "put-away."

How do you hit a volley?
1. Stand in a *balanced* position with your feet shoulder width apart and your weight slightly forward (on the balls of your feet). Flex your knees.
2. Hold your paddle up at all times at a height between your waist and chest (remember my admonition to *"See the paddle!"*)
3. *Believe* that you are confident, and strong, and able, and alert, and *project* that attitude toward your opponents!
4. Track the motion of the ball with your eyes from the moment it leaves your opponent's paddle.
5. Flip the paddle face to a forehand or backhand position (depending on where the ball is coming toward you).
6. Hold your arm firmly and minimize your swing. Instead, *block* the oncoming shot and *direct* the ball back in the desired direction by moving your forearm and paddle approximately 12-18 inches forward. *Snap* the ball toward your opponent as though you are punching it forward.
7. Try to change the angle of your volley so that you don't return the ball directly at your opponent's paddle and

make it easy for them to make their next shot. (This may involve snapping your wrist.)

8. Try to catch your opponent off guard by *angling* the ball toward their backhand side, or their feet, or toward the opponent's partner.
9. Be careful not to step forward to cross the NVZ line with your feet (as that would constitute a "fault").
10. Immediately return your paddle to the "up" or "ready" position in front of you.
11. Expect a swift volleying return from your opponent, so be alert.
12. Remember that the harder you hit a shot toward your opponent, most of the time it will return even more quickly to you.
13. A volley exchange can also form the basis for a drop shot (dink) into the opponent's Non Volley Zone, in order for you to wait for an opponent to make an error.

*Source: This material was adapted from Mary Littlewood, Pickleball Fundamentals, and Prem Carnot, Smart Pickleball.

THE THIRD SHOT DROP*

I have previously introduced and stressed the critical importance of the Serve, and the Return of Serve. Unless those two shots are completed successfully, volleys cannot take place (unless you violate the "Double Bounce" rule!).

After the ball is returned to either member of the serving team, those players will often find that both of their opponents are now at the NVZ line (or approaching it), and therefore in a strong offensive position. However, both members of the serving team are usually still back at the baseline and face the challenge of moving forward. One method of accomplishing this is for the serving team to execute the "**third shot drop**" to give them time to move to the NVZ and set up the dinking game. This is a *very* important pickleball shot to use.

The **third shot drop**, when done properly, follows a trajectory that is lofted higher than a typical groundstroke such that its arc reaches its peak height on *your* side of the net (at about *your* NVZ line) and then drops just over the net into the opponent's non-volley zone. It might be ideal to aim it towards the player who made the return of serve, since s/he will likely be moving forward and not yet firmly planted at the NVZ (thus making it difficult for that person to hit it aggressively).

The keys to hitting a successful **third shot drop** are that it be a *soft* hit using a *lifting* motion with *controlled speed* (not a hard groundstroke) and that it not be hit too high (such that your opponent can smash the ball back at you). In effect, it is a low and intentionally short lob type of shot that peaks at about one's own NVZ line at a 5' height and drops softly into the opponent's NVZ. You should make a smooth, soft, controlled contact with the ball. It then requires that you and your partner move in tandem toward the NVZ (using your peripheral vision to assure that you progress forward together).

To make the shot, position your body as though you were about to hit a groundstroke by aiming your left shoulder (for right-handers) toward your opponent and leading with your left foot. Hit the ball with a slightly open (upward) paddle face and shift your weight toward your front foot. Follow through with your paddle after making contact. Allow the ball at least 12 inches of clearance beyond the net, and remember to aim (initially, before you develop more skill) for the middle of the court.

One good way to develop your skill in using this shot is to start at the NVZ line with your opponents across from you. Hit a dink to them, asking them to hit progressively deeper shots back to you as you cautiously retreat one step at a time while continuing to make longer and longer drop shots over the net. Do this until you are capable of making the drop shot while standing at the baseline. Monitor your success by the frequency with which your drop shots land in the opponent's NVZ. Then start practicing "moving up" to the NVZ immediately after hitting a **third shot drop**.

You will eventually discover that "the **third shot (drop)** is a charm" and an important part of your "arsenal" of different shots. Remember: the **third shot drop** is not intended to be a winning shot but only a *set-up shot* to allow you to get into a dinking match.

*For those wanting visual examples of this shot, search Google using "pickleball **third shot drop**" and then looking for video results (e.g., Wes Gabrielson, or Picklepong Deb).

DINKING: THE SOFT GAME*

Why should you dink?

There are several reasons why players use the soft game. The most important one is that in order to get better, you want to play against better players. As you play against better players, it is critical that you do *not* give your opponent a ball with which they can hit a winning shot. This usually requires hitting a ball softly into the opponent's "kitchen" area (NVZ) by *dinking*. The dink shot is a lifted shot that is soft and/or low and bounces in the NVZ so that your opponent cannot do much else with it other than dink it back to you. If they were to try and smack this ball, it is so low and close to the net that it will likely either go out long or hit the net. Now it becomes a question of who is the best dinker—and the most patient player.

Average bangers (players that like to hit the ball hard and end the point now) do not like the dink (soft) game. *They don't want to have to dink the ball.* The soft game takes control and patience, two qualities most bangers do not have. If you and your partner are good at the soft game and are willing to both use it, you will generally beat the bangers because you can make them play the soft game. The first time you hit the ball softly into the NVZ, they can't bang the ball. Understand that the banger *wants* you to get into a hard-hitting battle with them so it can become a battle of who is the best hardest hitter. When you start dinking the ball it becomes a battle of who is the best dinker, and then *you* will have the advantage (if you have practiced this shot sufficiently).

How do you get into the soft game?

If you are the serving team, just hit the third shot softly into the kitchen, and the soft game is started. If you are the receiving team it is a little more difficult. The key now is to make sure that the serve return that you are going to hit does one of the following:

1) Goes to the backhand (weaker side) of your opponent.

2) Goes to the weaker of the opponents so they are not as able to overpower you.

3) Goes deep on the return. It is very hard to overpower you if the hard-hitting opponent has to hit the ball back at you from

the baseline. It just takes too much time for the ball to travel that distance. You should be waiting at the NVZ for this return and try to hit it back to the baseline area repeatedly. The opponents will get frustrated with each shot that comes back to them and each time they'll try and hit it harder and lower. After a couple of shots they will hit it into the net or out long.

After you get better, you will develop a drop shot with you standing at the NVZ with them banging away at the baseline. This is *sometimes* an effective shot, as now they don't know if you will return it back at their feet or drop it softly into the kitchen. (The problem with dropping it softly into the kitchen is that it brings your opponents up to the net.) The key is to get the serve return DEEP to them. If you hit it shallow (into "no man's land"), they will often be able to overpower you.

What do you do if an opponent errs and hits a dink that is too high?

You have at least three options. First, you can *drive* the ball directly toward them (see "Body Shots") and catch them by surprise. Second, you can hit a hard *smash* down toward their feet. Third, you can hit a soft *lob shot* that lands near the baseline (preferably over an opponent's non-dominant shoulder).

Pickleball at the higher levels is all about *controll aggression*. You must know when to hit hard and when to hit so. Above all, you must be a smart (and patient) player.

*Much of this discussion is drawn from material by Jeff Shank.

THE OVERHEAD SMASH (SLAM; "PUT-AWAY")

Definition:
The *overhead smash* is largely self-defining. It is a hard shot hit from well above the head aimed in a downward direction toward the opponent's feet or body. If done effectively its rapid velocity, sharp angle, and location of a target near the surface of the court make it extremely difficult for an opponent to anticipate and return it.

Procedure/mechanics:
An opportunity for an *overhead smash* arises when an opponent lofts a relatively soft shot that rises well above your head but within your outstretched paddle's reach. This is usually caused by a downward shot by your team, a "lifted" ball from the opponent, or simply a mishit by them. As soon as you see the ball coming you should move to a position that will place you slightly behind the ball and to its left (for a right-handed player) as you track its flight with your eyes. Turn your body so that your left shoulder partially faces the net, with your left foot ahead of your right foot and your weight shifted to the rear.

Extend your paddle arm high behind your right shoulder, with the paddle cocked at your wrist. As the ball approaches its apex above you, swing your paddle arm up and forward until contact is made with the ball as your paddle is behind and *on top of the ball* (angled moderately downward by as much as 45 degrees at the moment of impact). Shift your body weight forward in order to add additional force to the shot, and follow through in a downward arc. Be careful so as not to step into the NVZ when making an *overhead smash*, or your efforts will be wasted!

The goal of the *overhead smash* is to capitalize on an infrequent opportunity to definitively end a rally and put away the shot. It should be executed while under control but with an attitude of an assertive hit. If possible, aim for the middle of the court or use an angled shot to make it more difficult for your opponent to block it successfully. (Note that you can also make a backhanded *overhead smash* when you don't have time to move under the ball properly, but this shot generally has less force behind it.)

Difficulties:
Typical problems encountered in attempting an *overhead smash* include:
1. hitting the ball into the net (caused by impatience and not letting the ball come to you, or by angling your paddle downward too sharply),
2. hitting the ball too long or too wide (caused by trying to hit the ball too hard or a failure to aim to the middle), or
3. not getting enough force behind the ball (often caused by a fear of hitting an opponent, similar to the "Minnesota Nice" syndrome).

Defending against the overhead smash:
1. Don't loft the ball if at all possible so as to prevent a smash.
2. Keep your paddle ready.
3. Anticipate the downward angle of the shot and bend down low to receive it.
4. Consider turning your body to protect your face and front.
5. Consider retreating carefully a few steps (in concert with your partner).
6. If you successfully get your paddle on the ball, angle the paddle upward so as to have a chance of returning the ball over the net (even lobbing it).

THE LOB SHOT

Definition: The *lob shot* is a deep lofted shot usually hit off a bounce. The objective is to force your opponents back to their baseline, while buying time for you to advance to the NVZ line if you aren't already there. The most important factor is to view a lob as being a *soft lift of the ball*, as opposed to the crisp, brisk shot used in a groundstroke from the baseline.

Types of lobs: The lob shot can be useful either defensively or offensively. The *defensive lob* comes into play when the team returning the serve hits it sharply deep into the server's court such that you have little time to hit a returning groundstroke. As the opponents follow their deep shot to the net, you may wish to attempt to loft the ball over their outstretched paddle and drive them back or force an error.

The defensive lob can also be used when you are forced off the court by a wide serve or shot and both opponents are already at the NVZ line. A deep lob allows you to "reset the point" and get back on court.

The *offensive lob* is used at a crucial point during a dinking exchange to surprise the opponent. When both teams are up at the net, one player suddenly lofts the ball deep to an opponent's backhand side of the court. This is especially effective if an opponent is physically slow to react, or if the opponents will be confused over who should take the lob.

Effective lobs must clear the opponent's outstretched paddle, land in the court, not be too high, and be as deep as possible. Lobs should not be used too frequently, or they will lose the effectiveness of a surprise. Do not try lobs if you can't execute them well, for you and your partner will suffer the consequences— a hard smash back at you. Remember—there is only about 6-8 feet of space to work with behind the typical opponent, and even less behind a tall/agile one.

Defending the Lob: There are three main tactics to use when an opponent lobs over your head.

1. Simply admire their skills and call out "Nice shot!" to them while letting the ball bounce harmlessly behind you. (No bones are broken with this approach.)
2. You can *turn* your body and take quick steps toward your baseline, while keeping your eyes on the flight of the ball. Then hit a return shot—either while the ball is in the air or upon its bounce, and either via a low groundstroke or by a high defensive lob that gains you sufficient time to return to the NVZ.
3. Call out "Help" or "Yours" or "Take it" to your partner, who then cuts diagonally back toward the baseline to retrieve and hit the ball while you are moving sideways to take your partner's position on the other side of your court (while announcing "Switch" to alert him/her that s/he should remain on your previous side of the court (after hitting the ball. If you do this, however, make sure that you reverse positions after the ball is no longer in play or you will be penalized on the next point for being in the incorrect position.) And remember: when lobbing the pickleball, it is usually better to lob too high than to lob too low (because if the ball is too low or too short, your opponent will then likely slam the ball back at your team for a probable winner—and possibly a body bruise for you or your partner).

THE "LET IT GO" (NON) SHOT*

Free (easy) points. Oftentimes your opponent will offer you a "free" point by hitting the ball into the net or blatantly out of bounds. *Opponent-made errors help you win points and games*, so let them do so!

However, opponents also may hit balls that will prove to land just outside the sidelines or baseline. If you are too anxious or are unsure, players often mistakenly "save" their opponents by flailing at a potential "out" ball. *Let it go!* This is a prime opportunity for your partner to help you (and for you to help them) by calling out "Bounce it" or "Let it go" or at least "Watch it."

Similarly, you will undoubtedly encounter "bangers" in some future pickleball games—players who hit almost every ball at high speed with every fiber of their body and all their strength. Many of these balls will sail out of bounds on their own *if you let them do so*. What should you do? *Get out of its way*. Move. Turn. Duck. Avoid touching the ball.

The bottom line: Learn to recognize the speed and height of balls hit toward you and *let the lines be your friends!*

A strategic song. Do you remember the wintry Christmas song, "Let it snow"? If you know the tune, you can sing these opening lyrics (which I've adapted to the game of pickleball):

"Oh, my partner is so delightful,
but my opponent is very frightful,
and since he won't hit the ball slow
Let it go! Let it go! Let it go!"

He hits the ball at me so hard,
So I must be on my best guard,
My partner yells "No! No! No!"
Let it go! Let it go! Let it go!"

(Chorus)
When I finally learn to duck,

It changes my pickleball luck,
The advice was oh so very curt,
So nevermore will I get hurt!

If the ball is likely going out,
Then "Bounce it" I really should shout,
I will frustrate my worthy foe
By simply saying, *"I'll just let it go!"*

*Source: The early portion of this discussion is adapted from Jeff
Shank, *Pickleball Tipbits* #186. The words to the tune are my own.

CHAPTER 4

Improving Your Game

PRACTICE GROUPS

The Problem.

Have you been playing for some time and not really been able to progress as some others have? Have you wanted to play with the next level of players but you feel somewhat out of place or overmatched when you do? Do you want to feel like you belong and not rely on the kindness of others for being included? Do you feel you are just not up to their caliber? If that's you, you are not alone.

That feeling can come at any time in your playing development; it's not just when you first start after a "PB 101" introductory class. It occurs whenever you want to progress from one rating level to the next! (See, for example: Pickleball Ratings, and also Pickleball Self-Ratings.)

Start Now.

You need to have a plan that has a specific goal within the overall process of making your game better. You can't expect to immediately add multiple improvements to your game but you've got to start somewhere—and the sooner the better.

Resistance.

One answer lies in the formation of a *Practice Group*. Many players, however, are passively not interested, and some *actively* resist doing so because of:

1. *Competition for one's time* (yards to mow, gardens to tend, houses to paint, visitors to entertain, or travel plans to make);
2. *Bad memories of the word "practice"* (exhaustion after sports practices, boredom with clarinet lessons, even injuries incurred at a practice session);
3. *Lethargy* (practice demands not only time but effort, and we have just limited amounts of energy available);
4. *Discouragement* (initial attempts to change a behavior often result in *diminished* performance before improvement sets in);

5. *Lack of commitment* (practice is hard work, and sometimes we are unwilling to place a high priority on getting better).

A Positive Approach.
You can start to form a Practice Group by identifying others with similar goals and motivations—preferably a total of at least four persons who have skills roughly equal to your own and are willing to make a commitment that might extend anywhere from one to multiple sessions across several weeks. Attempt to find a common day and time (and place) on which to meet.

Start a discussion of specific goals along with candid statements of your current skill levels. Voice your commitment levels out loud to each other. Ask yourselves what other resources (i.e., pickleball books, magazines, instructional videos) are available to you as possible substitutes or complements to your effort to improve. Set aside regular blocks of time (60-90 minutes) for the sessions.

Embrace the idea that *the best way to achieve a higher level of skill and greater consistency is through repetitive drilling.* Obtain suggestions for drills from experienced players. Promise to praise each other for identified successes. Finally, *consider asking a coach to help your group,* since an objective observer can often provide valuable insights and feedback for improvement.

PICKLEBALL RATINGS

An extremely useful way to identify your current skill level and chart a path to improvement is to be aware of the standard explanations for what constitutes each level of pickleball achievement. There are nine defined categories, as follows:

1.0 **Novice.** These persons are totally new to pickleball, and may have heard about it or seen it played. They have minimal knowledge of the game.

1.5 Beginner. These players have learned the basic rules, are learning how to serve and keep score, and can occasionally sustain short rallies with players of equal ability. They are starting to develop a forehand stroke, but occasionally fail to return (or even miss) easy balls. They exhibit obvious weaknesses in their strokes. They have played a few games and are starting to internalize the scoring system and how to make line calls.

2.0 **Emerging Beginner.** These players demonstrate the basic shot strokes such as the forehand, backhand, volleys, overheads, and serves but exhibit weaknesses in most strokes. They are in the initial stages of making an effort to be more aggressive and occasionally move up to the non-volley zone. They are aware of the existence of lobs and dinks. They are becoming familiar with proper court positioning.

2.5 Advanced Beginner. These players make longer-lasting but slow-paced rallies; they make most easy volleys and occasionally use some backhand strokes. Their knowledge of the rules has improved but is not yet comprehensive. Their court coverage is weak but improving. They have not yet fully embraced the need to maximize play at the NVZ line. Their strokes lack control when they try for direction, depth, or power on their shots. They are becoming aware of the importance of the "soft game." They clearly embrace standard guidelines for the safety of themselves and others.

3.0 **Intermediate.** These players are becoming more consistent with their serves and service returns. They are beginning to attempt offensive and defensive lobs but with little or no success. They are fairly consistent with hitting medium-paced shots. They are beginning to experiment with dinks and lobs on a regular basis as an important part of the game but may not understand when they should be used. They still need to work on an increased degree of direction, depth, and power in their shots. They may lack sufficient athleticism to move swiftly around the court.

3.5 **Advanced Intermediate.** These players have dependable strokes, including directional control and depth on both the forehand and backhand sides. They can use lobs, overheads, approach shots, and volleys with success and they occasionally force errors when serving or returning service. Teamwork in doubles is evident. Rallies may be lost due to impatience. They are beginning to use Third Shot Drops, dinks, and a mixture of pace and angles in their game. They are learning to anticipate opponents' shots; they can cover lobs over their partner's head; they exhibit some aggressive net play; and they are exhibiting the consistent use of some strategy and teamwork. These players are not intimidated when they are the target of opponent smashes, and successfully return some of those.

4.0   **Advanced.** These players have developed their use of power and spin, can successfully execute all shots, can control depth of their shots, and can handle pace. They have sound footwork, understand strategy, and can adjust to the techniques of their opponents on the court. They have begun playing in advanced and open level tournaments. They fully comprehend all the rules of the game and can play accordingly. They regularly use Third Shot strategies (drop shots, lobs, and fast-paced ground strokes). They consistently adapt their play to the strengths and weaknesses of their partners, and communicate effectively with them.

4.5 **Advanced Tournament.** These players serve with power and accuracy and can vary their choice of approach. They demonstrate understanding of the importance of "keeping the ball in play" during rapid volley exchanges. They have mastered a wide variety of shots, can effectively block hard groundstrokes, and make good choices in shot selection. They can force opponents into making errors. They are dependable in stressful situations, and keep unforced errors to a minimum while capitalizing on errors made by their opponents.

5.0 **National Champion.** These players have all the skills and experience to compete at the highest level and have proven themselves capable repeatedly by winning medals at national tournaments. They have superb athletic ability, quickness, agility, court sense, and raw athleticism that separate them from their opponents.

PICKLEBALL SELF-RATINGS

In addition to the nine broad descriptions of player rating categories from 1.0 to 5.0 shown on the previous pages, the USAPA has developed skill assessment forms. These can be used for *self*-rating purposes, and also for use by experienced *rating teams* to provide developmental feedback to aspiring players. As you might expect, the standards for each of the specific criteria are increasingly higher as a player progresses across the nine levels. A sample form for 3.0 players can be seen at *https://www.usapa.org/wp-content/uploads/2015/04/Skill-Assessment-3.0.pdf*

The various forms focus on categories such as these:
1.   Percentage of serves that are good.
2.   Presence of foot-faults during serving.
3.   Percentage of forehand service returns that are good.
4.   Percentage of backhand service returns that are good.
5.   Percentage of forehand volleys that are good.
6.   Percentage of backhand volleys that are good.
7.   Presence (absence) of non-volley zone foot faults.
8.   Athleticism (mobility, quickness, hand-eye coordination).
9.   Knowledge of the rules, scoring, and correct server.
10.   Quickness of approach to the non-volley zone line.
11.   Demonstrates a wide variety of shots.
12.   Initiates and maintains a sustained dink exchange at the net.
13.   Uses a forehand and backhand lob when appropriate.
14.   Adjusts to differing ball speeds.
15.   Sustains short volley sessions with placement and control.
16.   Uses differently-paced shots to advantage.
17.   Consistently returns lower shots over the net.
18.   Uses deeper and higher returns of serve to approach the net quicker.
19.   Teamwork in using court strategies and partner communication.
20.   Avoidance of hitting "out" balls.
21.   Demonstration of patience during rallies.
22.   Ability to hit to coverage gaps.

These categories are then used to rate a player on a 4-point scale, where 0=Not able to execute, 1=Tried but very poorly executed and needs work, 2=Good basic form but needs additional work, and 3=Solid, consistent performance. As a player strives to attain the next rating level, she or he must demonstrate most or all of the skills defined at the lower level, as well as those identified at the next higher level.

Self-assessment, if done objectively, forms a strong foundation for self-improvement through additional (guided) practice. The specific on-court behaviors listed above are much more valuable than broad intentions simply to "become a better player." All players are urged to identify their relative shortcomings and strive to turn these into strengths by using these forms as a guide.

CLIMBING THE LADDER TO SUCCESS

Many beginner pickleball players, once they have become "addicted" to pickleball, want to know what it will take to become more proficient at the sport. At the risk of great oversimplification, a "newbie" might consider the path to success as a series of rungs on a ladder, in which none of the steps should be neglected. Starting at the bottom and working the way up, the following areas could be consider as important:

1. **Rules**. All games have rules, and pickleball is no different. Rules exist for a reason, and there is no excuse for not knowing them. It's a great place to start!

2. **Basics**. These include paddle selection, the grip, scoring, knowing how to move up to the non-volley zone line, a variety of elements related to courtesy, etiquette, and good sportsmanship, prescriptions for personal safety, and recognizing the importance of hitting your shots toward the middle of the court.

3. **Shot development**. No one wants to be a "one shot wonder," so it is imperative to learn how to hit a wide variety of shots—the serve, forehand and backhand groundstrokes, dinks, third shot drops, lobs, drop shots, and overhead smashes—and when to use them.

4. **Controlled aim**. It's often said that the more specific your target is, the more likely you are to hit it. In the very beginning of the journey to skilled play, it seems adequate to simply get the ball back over the net. Later, however, it becomes increasingly important to *place* your shots where you want them to go, and thus control becomes paramount.

5. **Consistency**. Closely aligned with control comes consistency. This means that the level of accuracy (reliability) improves in a number of areas. Primary among them are the frequency of getting the serve in, the frequency of making successful returns of serve, and the success of your dinking game.

6. **Position**. This starts with being in the right place on the court at the right time. It involves moving one's feet,

bending low to better see the oncoming ball, and using geometry to place angled shots against your opponents.

7. **Teamwork.** Unless you choose to play exclusively in singles events, coordinating one's actions with your teammate is a vital need. This includes advance discussions regarding strategy and tactics, ongoing communication during the course of a game, and synchronizing one's movements with your partner.

8. **Power.** With regard to developing and using power in one's shots, a player might initially believe that "More is better" (and have gained this belief through watching pickleball "bangers" hit every shot as hard as they can). However, it is actually more accurate to say, "Less is more." Instructors and pros alike consistently stress that most shots only require about 80% of your potential power. Beyond that level, the probability of errors increases dramatically.

As you "climb" these eight rungs, you will increase your chances of attaining new "heights" in your pickleball game!

NO MAN'S LAND

Dictionary definition: This is an unoccupied region between opposing forces that is dangerous to enter or remain in due to danger, fear, or uncertainty.

Military metaphor: Picture, in your mind, two enemies safely situated some distance apart who have informally established a temporary truce that is interrupted occasionally and sporadically with mortar fire that is only strong enough to land in the space between the two sides. Would you want to wander unknowingly into this zone? Would you want to "camp out" in such an area? Would you not want to be warned to stay *out* of this region when you first arrive at your assigned station? Even if your commander told you to participate in a raid of the enemy position, would you not want to at least *minimize* the amount of time spent in this "no man's land" as you approach your target?

A pickleball interpretation: In pickleball, this is a space on both sides of the net, roughly bounded by the two sidelines in width, and perhaps 7-8 feet in depth, sitting midway between the baseline and the non-volley zone (NVZ). This is informally known as **"no man's land"**—an area impossible to avoid on your way to the strongly advantageous position of being "at the net," but in which you should minimize your time.

Why would you wish to avoid "no man's land" on the pickleball court? The answer is simple: if you stand there for more than a second or two, it is highly likely that your opponent will hit a shot at your feet. These shots are not only *difficult* to return over the net, but usually force a "lifted" return that allows your opponent to smash the ball back at you again.

When you stand in "No Man's Land" at midcourt you are neither "here" (at the highly-desirable NVZ line) nor "there" (standing back at the baseline). As a consequence:

1. You are limited in your ability to engage in the dinking element of the game.

2. You are more likely to miss on making smashes/slams on short high balls (that are normally "gifts" to you from your opponent).

3. It is more difficult for you to return deep shots from your opponent because their shots are landing at your feet and if you do hit a return it is likely to be a lofted one that gives them the opportunity to slam it back at you.

4. Your opponent has more tactical options to use (e.g., short drops over the net, short angled shots to the side, deep shots to your feet, or well-aimed shots to your (presumably weaker) backhand side.

How can you avoid becoming trapped in "no man's land"?

1. *Commit yourself* to attaining a position of strategic strength (at the NVZ line) as soon as possible during *every point played.* This is an assertive mental attitude.

2. *Move forward* immediately after striking a return of serve, using the extended pull of your stroke to assist your physical advance.

3. If necessary, *attain your goal in progressive steps* by always stopping your advance as soon as your opponent strikes the ball, using the "split step" technique to position your feet side by side and firmly planted before hitting your next shot (and then again advancing).

Can you *really* present any valid arguments for staying *in* "No Man's Land?"

GET TO THE NET (NVZ) AFTER RETURN OF SERVE

What does it mean to "get to the net?"

In one sense, the phrase is really a misnomer, since you should not normally be physically close (adjacent) to the net. The phrase simply directs a player who has just returned the serve to move forward (possibly in stages) until her/her feet are just *inches* behind the Non Volley Zone line.

Why might some players resist doing this?

There are several reasons, and each new player needs to introspectively examine their own possible resistance. For example:

1. Sometimes one's background (e.g., in tennis) has engrained the desirability of making multiple baseline shots and being successful.
2. Initially there might be fear of being so close to an opponent and getting hit by the ball.
3. It is possible that the distance to cover from baseline up to the NVZ line (15 feet) might appear challenging in just a few seconds' time.
4. Some players' personalities are inconsistent with being aggressive players.
5. New players may not realize how this can be achieved (but see below).
6. Players may not recognize the *advantages* of doing so (making dinks, smashes, offensive lobs, angled shots).

How does a new player accomplish "getting to the net?"

1. *Mentally* decide that it is advantageous to be at the net for volleying and smashing (i.e., "I see the logic of doing so.").
2. *Observationally* conclude that other (good) players do so consistently. (i.e., "I've watched videos of top players do this to their great benefit.).
3. *Physically* determine whether you can do so (i.e., "I have no handicap that prevents me from advancing in the way that my instructor recommends.").

4. *Attitudinally* resolve that you will do so (i.e., "I will commit to moving up after each time that I make a return of serve.").
5. *Practice* your new skill (i.e., "I will hit soft, high [lofted] returns of serve to give yourself additional time to get to the net.").
6. *Take long strides* or quick steps to shorten the time to get there. (If necessary, stop midway ("split-step") for one shot and then continue your advance.)
7. Once you get to the NVZ, *do not retreat*. (Hit firm volleys directed at your opponent's weaknesses, such as at their feet, backhand, body, or the "golden middle.")
8. *Monitor your success rate* (i.e., the frequency in which you attain the NVZ, such as 9 out of 10 times in a typical game).
9. *Seek help.* (Ask a partner, friend, or coach to provide reminders and a critique after you play a game.)

Conclusion:

Getting to the net consistently is one of the most valuable strategic lessons that a beginning pickleball player can learn and practice.

THE GOLDEN MIDDLE

Using the middle to your advantage.
Following the classic admonishment to "KISS" ("Keep It Simple, Stupid"), pickleball coaches everywhere urge players to focus on a single primary target area—the *golden middle of the opponents' court*. Why is this extremely valuable advice? There are several valid arguments for doing so, as follows:

1. The pickleball net (which is an obstacle in the path of the ball if it is hit on too low of an arc) is 36" high at the sidelines, but only *34" high at its middle*. In other words, the barrier represented by the net is smaller in the middle and this makes it easier for the ball to pass over it. Why not use this to your advantage, by making fewer errors there?

2. Shots made "down the middle" may be out of reach by both opponents if they are too far apart, resulting in a "hole" between them and an easy point for your team.

3. Any time you aim your shot in the middle of your opponents, it may cause confusion between them. If so, they may *both* swing at the ball hit by you, or alternatively *neither one of them* may attempt to strike the ball. This produces a "free point" for the serving team.

4. Aiming for the middle is a much safer shot than it is to attempt placing a shot down one of the sidelines. Coaches preach never taking a shot that you can't make 80% of the time, and the shot down the middle has the least risk of being "out" compared to sideline shots.

Defending against shots to the middle.

If your opponents have received the same instruction and coaching as you have, surely they will attempt to attack the middle frequently, too. How can you defend against this? In simple terms, *cover (protect; defend) the middle!* Here are some suggestions on how to do this:

1. *Talk to your partner before the game begins.* Decide, based on several factors, who will take the shots that

are directed to the middle of your court—and how far into the deuce (even) court they will reach (e.g., 6-12 inches? 1-2 feet?). Then honor that commitment. It is especially important for the player on the right side of the court to "back off" and give the forehand player the latitude to take the shots down the middle. One national gold medalist/instructor (Robert Elliott) even suggested that the player in the right side court should consciously move *away* from the centerline in order to give the forehand player room to roam.

2. *Similarly, talk to each other during the course of play.* Use simple words of communication such as "Yours" or "Mine" or "Take it" to help clarify—in the heat of battle—what role each player should take.

Note that effective coverage of the middle (effectively forming a defensive "wall") may soon discourage your opponents from continuing that strategy, and force them to try other riskier alternatives (such as lobbing, or dinking, or low-probability shots down the sideline). Now you need to be prepared to defend against those, too.

UNFORCED ERRORS

Definition:

An *UnForced Error* (**UFE**) is a shot that is hit wide, short (into the net), long (beyond the baseline), or that sets up an opponent's sharp volley or smash. It is safe to assert that most recreational pickleball games (e.g., those played by players rated at 3.5 or less) are not won because of spectacular shots, but are lost because of simple mistakes made. In general, *the fewer unforced errors you make, the better you (and your team) will perform.*

The lesson from this is simple—just get the ball back over the net *one more time than your opponents do.* Sometimes this requires you to play defensive pickleball for a few shots, while patiently waiting for your opportunity to hit a winner.

Reasons for UFERS:

There are many possible explanations for the existence of UFERS, including:

1. Failure to have a specific target for each shot;
2. Hitting into an opponent's strength (e.g., the player's forehand);
3. Being too impatient (wanting to end the rally with the next stroke);
4. Taking unnecessary risks (e.g., attempting to "paint the lines" with your shots);
5. Taking your eyes off the ball and looking ahead to your target;
6. Trying to hit all shots with maximum power;
7. Not being in the correct position on the court or failure to adjust your position;
8. Attempting shots which you have not practiced adequately;
9. Not holding your paddle properly for the attempted shot;
10. Failure to bend your knees (get down low) or turn one's body so that your non-dominant shoulder points toward your target.

Likely Results of UFERS:
1. Loss of the upper hand during a rally;
2. Loss of the point;
3. Loss of the game;
4. Loss of momentum;
5. Loss of your partner's trust in your decision-making
6. Loss of your own confidence.

Collectively, these consequences will likely cause either you or your partner to mutter the Scandinavian expression of "Uffda!" (or something worse) because of disgust or dismay with your performance.

How to Reduce or Eliminate UFERS:
1. Monitor your current frequency of UFERS.
2. Set a goal for reducing UFERS (e.g., "I will make 97% successful serves.").
3. Cut back on your power shots (for example, using only 80-90% of your strength, vs. the current level).
4. Be selective when you go for outright "winners."
5. Be more conservative in your shot selection.
6. *Think* when you play pickleball.

CHAPTER 5

Adding Skills to Your Repertoire

TEAMWORK

It is safe to assert that the vast majority of pickleball court time is spent in the context of doubles (vs. singles) play. Unfortunately, many players lack formal experience in the concept of successful play as doubles partners. In a typical scenario, two strangers or casual acquaintances are thrown together to form a "team" on the PB court and expected to coordinate their efforts.

Teamwork.

A *team* is a collection of two or more individuals (preferably with complementary skills) who apply and coordinate their respective abilities, efforts, and communication skills in an attempt to achieve a challenging common objective (in this case, a single point or eventually a "win"). We have all heard the simplistic and overworked cliché, *"There is no 'I' in T.E.A.M."* Unfortunately, not every pickleball player acts in accord with this maxim.

So what does it look like when two players fail to think and act like a team? One example is when each player takes a "this side (of the centerline is *my* side, and that side is *your* side" perspective, with both persons simply defending their own side of the court and no one guarding the "golden middle." The other extreme is the presence of the "ball hog" (to be discussed in the next entry), a behavior that is equally dysfunctional. Another example is when one partner continually critiques the other player after almost every shot, or displays demeaning facial expressions and negative body language. Another possible consequence is when two partners run into each other or hit each other's hands while simultaneously attempting to make a shot. In summary, it is simply not fun to play with someone who is not interested in teamwork, even if every game is won by a score of 11-0.

Team-oriented behaviors.

Note that one of the criteria for achieving a 3.5 rating or higher in pickleball is *the evident demonstration of teamwork*. What does this consist of? Consider behaviors such as these:

1. Advance determination of who will cover "shots to the middle."
2. Sharing insights and observations about opponent strengths and weaknesses, wind direction, or the presence of a left-handed opponent.
3. Essential communication between partners during play, such as "mine" or "yours," "take it," "no" (or "out"), "bounce it," or "go up/get back." Good teammates know that it is much better to over-communicate than to lose a point (or a game) due to *failure* to communicate.
4. Prior discussion regarding how to handle lobs (e.g., yelling "switch" and exchanging sides on a seamless basis).
5. Moving up to, and back from, the NVZ together as a team.
6. Moving left and right together if one partner is drawn off the court. Maintain a consistent distance between you and your partner (perhaps 6-8 feet, depending on your mutual wingspan and agility).
7. Forgiving or ignoring your partner's errors, and providing positive feedback for good shots.
8. Having fun together. For example, frequent gold medalists Jennifer Lucore and Alex Hamner are not just excellent players, but they also enjoy each other's company, tease each other, and joke around.

Conclusion.

Maybe there is not only *one* "I" in T.E.A.M., but *two* "I's." However, both "I's" must be coordinated and synchronized for the team to reach its full potential.

THE BALL HOG

What is a ball hog?

Let's return to the definition of a team-- *a collection of two or more individuals (preferably with complementary skills) who apply and coordinate their respective abilities, efforts, and communication skills in an attempt to achieve a challenging common objective.* What happens when one pickleball player *neglects* that definition, and acts as though there *is* an 'I' in T.EA.M.? At its best, the team may still win if the player involved is truly a star (characterized by the phrase, "Everyone hates a ball hog, but they all love a scorer"). At its worst, any satisfaction derived from playing together may be lacking for the teammate(s). In general, it is not fun playing with a *ball hog—a player that constantly overshadows his/her partner and oversteps the bounds defining a team-oriented partner.* According to Wikipedia, a ball hog is a derisive terms that describes unacceptable behavior that is often detrimental to a team's cohesiveness and overall success. In addition, *ball-hogging is often considered to be unsportsmanlike.*

Ball Hog examples.

Several years ago I observed a tournament of advanced-caliber mixed doubles teams. One team consisted of a male (rated at 4.5) who was a former rugby player in England—a brawny and physically fit but chauvinistic person. His female partner (rated at 4.0) was quick on her feet and obviously experienced and capable. However, the egotistical male roamed all over the entire court and clearly took at least *90% of all the shots*—an incredible statistic! I was shocked at this imbalance, and could only wonder how his *partner* felt that day. To make it more personal, how do *you* feel when you play with a *"ball hog"* like the one described here?

In another context, I recall the (possibly apocryphal) story of basketball phenomenon Wilt Chamberlain when he first arrived at Kansas University. Because of his 7'1" physical attribute and scoring ability, Wilt began the practice season as a *ball hog*, demanding the ball from his teammates and immediately taking all the shots. His coach, Phog Allen, taught him an important lesson by pulling Wilt's four teammates from the court and telling Wilt he was on his own to dribble, shoot, rebound, and defend. Wilt soon discovered the futility of this requirement, and learned to value the contributions of his teammates to his own ultimate success. Again, *"There is no 'I' in T.E.A.M."* (A more recent example of a ball hog in the world of professional basketball is allegedly Kobe Bryant, who is notorious for demanding and keeping and shooting the ball.)

Why do pickleball players act like ball hogs?
There are several possible explanations, including:
1. They have not "bought into" the definition and characteristics of being a team.
2. They are simply selfish, and only concerned about *individual* success.
3. They believe that their teammates are inferior and therefore they must compensate for their inabilities.
4. Their teammates *allow* them to hog the ball.
5. We live in an era where "star" players are idolized.

How *do* you handle a ball hog?
Advance negotiation of roles (for example, "Who will cover the middle?") will prove fruitful. Reminders during a game (e.g., "Hey, I can reach those shots with my forehand") can be useful. Or take an official time out to suggest a change in partner behavior before it perpetuates itself. And if all else fails, simply refuse to play with ball hogs in the future. Eventually, they will get the message.

SHADOWING

Normally, team players in a doubles match coordinate their efforts so that they move together (they synchronize their position on the court, as though they are dance partners). They stay at a relatively constant distance apart (i.e., about 7-8 feet). This is termed **shadowing**—two people moving similarly just as though they are connected by a cord. This is a strong team position and helps them form a defensive "wall." Shadowing applies to movements forward and backward, as well as from side to side (laterally) and allows partners to control (minimize) the opening between them.

Failure to engage in shadowing.

It is important to note that if one player acts independently so as to move haphazardly or sporadically, this makes it *much* more difficult for the other partner! This is especially true if one partner relinquishes his/her valued position at the NVZ line and takes several steps backward to hit a ball while standing in "no man's land." Can you imagine what the self-descriptive monologue would sound like from the haphazard player if he/she would verbalize their play-by-play? It might go something like this—"I'm backing up now. I'm rushing to the NVZ line again. Oops, I got caught in no man's land. Now I'm going to back up again." The player's partner would be totally confused!

It is imperative that each player stay generally within the peripheral vision of his/her partner, or else the "team" becomes fragmented and frustration ensues. In short, the athleticism and agility that often helps a player succeed in a singles match can become highly *dysfunctional* during a doubles match.

Disciplined movement.

Should players move during a rally on the court? Of course they should, but it should be somewhat planned, controlled, and disciplined. Pro player/teacher/coach Sarah Ansboury has asserted that most recreational players move *too much* during a game. As a consequence, they find themselves out of position for their next shot and unprepared to respond because they are not fully balanced. Furthermore, players who are backing up as they attempt a groundstroke (or smash) find that they lose a substantial amount of power for that shot, and often hit the ball into the net.

A perfect example of the need for controlled movement and coordination between partners occurs when both players have achieved a "strong" position side-by-side at the NVZ. As the ball is bouncing on the opponent's court (left, middle, or right side, and either short or deep), both partners need to re-position themselves slightly to prepare for the most likely return shot. If the ball has gone to the left side of the opponent's court, the player on the odd (left) side should shift to his/her left to cover shots down the line, and vice versa for balls on the right side of the court. In the meantime, the player on the even (right) side of the court shifts toward the middle to cover sharply angled shots from the left, or shifts closer to the sideline to cover down-the-line shots from an opponent preparing to strike the ball on the right.

Synchronize your efforts.

To summarize, *think of yourself as a synchronized team* (no matter how temporary the relationship is). Act in a predictable way. Don't dance around needlessly. Stay within easy eyesight of your partner. Coordinate your efforts by *shadowing* your partner's movements.

RE-SET THE POINT!

While playing pickleball, many things can happen that put you (and your team, in a doubles match) on the defensive. For example:

1. Your opponent hits a deep lob that you can barely reach;
2. Your opponent sends a forceful shot that almost gets by you before you can get your paddle on it;
3. The ball hits the net and drops over such that you can only just barely reach it inside the Non Volley Zone;
4. A member of the opposing team hits a sharply-angled shot that draws you a step or more outside your own court in order to return the shot.

Overreaction.

Unfortunately, when most recreational players find themselves in one of these situations, there is a tendency to panic and attempt a desperate "winning" shot in return. This typically occurs while you are in motion, or out of position, or off balance, or outside the entire court. In effect, you are tempted to try to *win the point* rather than try to re-establish a neutral position—and it occurs from a position of weakness (or at least defensiveness).

Desperation.

The scenario described above happens numerous times on the pickleball court. Perhaps most glaring is when a player attempts to make a winning shot from a ball that has not bounced high enough to rise to net height. Instead of awaiting a better opportunity, the impatient individual "goes for a winner" and hits the ball into the net. POINT LOST!

Patience is needed.

The remedy for this situation stems from a useful admonition provided by national medalist Robert Elliott during a "Play with the Pros" event held in The Villages, Florida. He recommended that players try **to re-set the point** when they are in trouble. This means that your best strategy is to *buy yourself some* *time to get back into a neutral (or even positive) position on the court.* It basically suggests that if your opponent has you on the defensive, then the best thing you can do is to re-establish yourself in a neutral position through gaining some time (often by using a lobbed return instead of a hard smash or a dink.) Admittedly, this requires a certain amount of patience as well as the ability to (temporarily) throttle down your own competitive spirit and desire to win…now! In other words, you should focus on playing each point well enough to *get back into it* if the situation requires you and your partner to do so.

Re-set the point.
    The lesson is simple in concept but more difficult to implement during the heat of "battle." *Don't always try for an immediate winner—especially when the ball you are hitting is below net level.* **Re-set the point**. This recommendation ties in closely with one of the "Seven P's of Pickleball" discussed later in this book under Chapter VI—the need to *be patient.*

THE "AROUND THE POST" (ATP) SHOT

One of the most distinctive (but infrequently used in recreational play, except at advanced levels) shots is the one that goes around (outside) the net post and lands deeply in the opponent's court. The opportunity for this shot typically occurs when an opponent hits a sharply-angled dink (or smash) that draws a player well off the side of the court. At this time, most players will simply try to "reset the point" by hitting back to the middle of the opponent's court, hitting a cross-court dink, or making a defensive lob (to give them sufficient time to return to the court). Alternatively, they could aggressively capitalize on the opportunity to hit the next shot *around the (net) post and into the opponents' backcourt*. I will abbreviate this as an ATP shot.

Is the ATP shot legal?

In a nutshell, "Yes, it is." More specifically, Rule 11.M (Shots Around the Net Post) says, "A player *may* return the ball around the outside of the net post." In addition, the rule clearly notes, "The ball does not need to travel back *over* the net," and since "there is no restriction to the height of the return, a player may return the ball around the net post *below* the height of the net." (Tennis has a similar rule, which Roger Federer notably displayed in a U.S. Open match.)

A secondary issue of interest is addressed in Rule ll.L3, which states, "The player is allowed to go around the net post and cross the imaginary extension line of the net *after the ball is hit*, so long as the player or any item he or she is/was wearing or carrying does not touch the opponent's court. (However) If the player goes around the net post and crosses the imaginary extension line of the net but does not make *contact* with the ball, a fault will be declared."

What are the advantages of making an ATP shot?

First, if successfully conducted, it is usually a surprise to a recreational player and thus catches him/her off guard. Second, the ATP shot is almost nonreturnable, since the ball is directed *behind* the opponent. Third, when a successful ATP shot is made, it provides a significant *adrenaline rush* for the person hitting it. That combination makes for a win-win-win situation for the player who completes such a shot.

What does it take to make an ATP shot?

It requires great anticipation coupled with an advanced mindset (a commitment) that tells you to "go for it." In addition, it is likely that a player with substantial speed, agility, and accuracy will have greater odds of success. Finally, this shot has a much greater likelihood of succeeding *if it has been practiced in advance via repetitive drills.*

How does a player defend against the ATP shot?

Most importantly, a defensive player needs to *be aware of* the *possibility* and *probability* of an opponent's ATP shot. Anticipate it whenever your opponent is forced wide of the court. When the opponent attempts the ATP shot, choose one of these three options:

1. Back up a bit to better intercept the shot, and then *drive the ball down the line* (close to it) before the opponent has an opportunity to return to the court.
2. Intercept the ball and hit a defensive lob over either of your opponents.
3. Hit a drop shot to catch your opponents off-balance as they return to the court.

For an illustration of the ATP shot see, for example, this website: http:www.pickleballchannel.com/around-net-post

ERNE SHOT

What is an Erne Shot?

It is a sharp volley that makes contact with the ball when it is extremely close to the plane of the net by a player positioned *outside* the court's sidelines. An Erne Shot can be done from either the forehand or backhand side and generally incorporates an element of surprise.

Reasons for its rarity.

Not for the faint of heart (or slow of feet), the *Erne Shot* is rarely seen in mid-level recreational play. Why? The first answer lies in the need for quick judgment followed by lightning-quick movement in order to perform it effectively. A second reason for its rarity is that 3.0-rated players only infrequently engage in extended dink rallies (which are usually a prerequisite for the Erne Shot). A third reason is that this shot is seldom presented or discussed in either printed materials on pickleball or in introductory classes.

What are the relevant rules to be aware of?

There are several, including the following:

• A player attempting an Erne Shot must establish both feet on the ground outside the NVZ if s/he has been in the NVZ immediately preceding the shot.

• After contacting the ball from outside the sideline, a player's momentum cannot carry him/her into the NVZ.

• The player may not make contact with the ball before it has crossed the plane of the net as it approaches him/her. (Don't reach into the opponent's non-volley zone to hit the ball, as this would be a fault.)

• The player *may* break the plane of the net on the follow-through.

• The player *may* go around the net post and cross the imaginary extension of the net as long as the player does not enter the opponent's actual court.

• The player cannot touch the net or post with his/her body or paddle before or after contact with the ball.

What are the three ways in which you can make an Erne Shot?
1. Slide (*sidestep*) your feet toward the sideline until you clear the NVZ boundary, and then move quickly forward to meet the oncoming ball. This is a 90-degree turn with greater distance involved, and usually takes longer for the player to complete the process.
2. Leap *over* the corner of the non-volley zone without touching any part of it and then hit the oncoming ball.
3. Step directly *through* the non-volley zone and then quickly establish *both* feet on the court outside the surface of the non-volley zone before making contact with the ball.

How do you *prevent* an opponent from hitting an Erne Shot?
Don't hit a predictable series (two or more) of high dinks close to the opponent's sideline and straight forward. This sets up a golden opportunity for your opponent to hit an Erne Shot!

POACHING

What is it?

Poaching is the act of one player (in doubles play) moving laterally and substantially across the court at the NVZ line to make a shot that would predictably have been returned by the player's partner. In other words, the poacher is making a more distinctive and more distant move beyond the "normal" practice of using a dominant forehand to take shots that are in the middle of the court.

Why is it done?

Poaching is usually done for one (or several) of four reasons:

• To capitalize on the surprise factor as a tactic that attempts to catch the opponents off guard,

• To capitalize on the unique assets and attributes of one partner (e.g., his or her speed, quickness, and agility; above-average height and associated reach; and/or physical strength).

• To compensate for the deficiencies of a poacher's partner (e.g., a partner who normally stays back at the baseline).

• To feed the ego of a presumably (or self-assessed) dominant player.

When is it done?

Poaching often occurs when the forehand player (the right-handed person who is currently on the left side of the court) moves across the court to his/her right to take a shot that is directed toward their partner. Alternatively, it could also be done with a backhand shot from the other side (or by a "southpaw" moving to his/her left from the right-hand court). The poaching player needs to be selective so as not to tip one's hand and leave his/her own side of the court unprotected. Further, *poaching can be done either spontaneously or as part of a planned strategy* based on previous signals sent to the poacher's partner.

What types of poachers are there?

One writer suggests that there are *compulsive (obsessive, or aggressive)* poachers (who do it at every opportunity) and *opportunistic* poachers (who do so infrequently and only when the moment clearly presents itself). Both types would benefit from discussing this strategy with their partner in advance.

What defensive tactics work best against an aggressive poacher?
There are at least three:
1. Aim most shots *at* the body or forehand side of the poacher's partner (i.e., away from the poacher, and out of his/her reach).
2. Aim shots *behind* the poacher as he/she moves (i.e., to his/her backhand side to catch the poacher off guard and teach him/her a lesson to "Stay Home!").
3. Aim shots toward the poacher's body and low (see: "Body Shots.")

Should *you* poach occasionally?
Yes! It is a "tool" that should be in every good player's bag of tricks. It also adds excitement to the game by creating suspense as to whether or not (and when) the poaching may occur. Keep your opponents guessing!

BODY SHOTS

Body shots—what are they?

Body shots, in a sophomoric college party environment, usually involve licking some salt off of a partner's body, drinking an ounce of tequila, and sucking on a slice of lime—and then doing this repeatedly. *Body shots*, in the course of a pickleball game however, are totally different; they *involve either hitting an opponent with your shot or being hit by your opponent's shot.*

Does it happen? Will it happen to you?

The answer to both questions is a resounding "Yes." In my experience, it is hard to find any PB player who has *not* been hit—multiple times—during the course of their playing career. Hits occur on the feet, ankles, legs, gut, chest, hands/wrist/arms, and on the head. Does a body shot hurt? Yes, it can sting. Does it injure? Rarely (fortunately). Unquestionably, the most dangerous hit to incur is one to the eyes, which is why many thoughtful players choose to wear protective safety glasses.

Why do body shots occur?

Three primary reasons are:

1. *The PB court is small,* and opponents are separated by a short distance (as little as 7-8 feet, if a shot bounces high and short just over the net and then is slammed during the return).

2. *Many players are capable of hitting very hard/fast shots.* Given the speed at which the ball travels, a defending player has only an instant in which to react.

3. *Some players fail to defend themselves adequately.* They may not have tracked the ball with their eyes, they may have been distracted or even fearful, or they simply may have failed to hold their paddle up at chest level to protect their bodies from a fast-moving ball.

Should a player ever aim for a body shot?

There are two answers to this question, as follows:

1. One PB clinic instructor gave this three-part advice "Hit them; Make them bleed; Finish them off." In short he was suggesting that a player might be able to intimidate the opponent effectively via a body shot. In addition, once you try to avoid hitting to someone's forehand or backhand, the options remaining are rather limited. Bluntly, body shots are quite effective because of the difficulty in defending against them.
2. Alternatively, no one (presumably) wishes to harm another (or be labeled as a "hit shot" specialist). Many body shots are unintentional, however, as it is nearly impossible to control one's aim so precisely as to avoid making an occasional body shot.

Conclusion.

Players are strongly advised to *anticipate* body shots by being alert to the possibility, *minimize* making them, and *protect yourself* from receiving them by holding your paddle high in front of you at all times.

DEFEATING THE PICKLEBALL "BANGERS"

What are "bangers?"

They are players who hit the ball as hard as they can every time they have an opportunity to do so, though usually it is from the baseline or deep in their own court. They have little or no respect for the soft game and rarely use it.

Understanding why bangers bang.

There are at least four explanations for the seemingly pervasive existence of bangers.

1. *Testosterone.* Most (but not all) of the bangers are male, and they act as though the masculine thing to do is to whack the ball as hard as they can (probably similar to what they would do in tennis, racquetball, table tennis, softball, or golf).

2. *Limited background.* It is possible that they have not received formal instruction in pickleball but only picked it up informally. Therefore, they may truly be unfamiliar with the intricacies of using soft shots and finesse.

3. *Immobility.* Some of the bangers may lack athleticism and be unable or unwilling to move very much on the court. For them, it is simpler to remain at the baseline and trade groundstrokes with their opponents.

4. *Success.* An opponent who is hitting the ball hard can be overwhelming to many beginners. This can produce a "Why change now?" attitude among the bangers when they cannot only win points but also intimidate their opponents (see "Testosterone," above).

Why do bangers win?

First, it is relatively easy to hit forehand and backhand groundstrokes—especially when beginners "feed the monster" by sending softly lofted balls to them. Second, non-bangers often contribute to the bangers' success by rescuing them (attempting to return shots that would have gone deep or wide and out of bounds). A good cliché to invoke here is simply, "If it's shoulder high, let if fly." A third reason is that lower-rated players may not yet have developed the capability to engage in successful blocking behaviors, as described below. Finally, there is no question that fear of facing a hard shot can be intimidating to a (beginner) player facing a banger.

How to counter a banger.

There are three primary ways to solve the banger problem—the third shot drop, and effective blocking (hard and soft).

1. The third shot drop, as discussed in Chapter 3, is an anticipatory defensive shot. It is designed to prevent your opponent from ever having the opportunity to hit shots firmly in the first place. After the serve and its return, a well-executed drop shot into the opponent's non-volley zone (NVZ) takes away the chance to bang it forcefully toward you. Instead, it effectively draws your opponent to the NVZ line to enter into a dinking game (see that discussion in Chapter 3).

2. There are two different blocking maneuvers you can use against bangers. The *hard block* uses the opponent's energy to return the ball to them as quickly as it was sent—preferably by a punch shot aimed at the banger's feet.

3. The soft block is a drop volley that dramatically slows the ball down and drops it into the opponent's NVZ—possibly catching the banger off guard.

WHAT'S MY ANGLE? (USING GEOMETRY TO GAIN AN ADVANTAGE)

Many years ago, on black and white television, Garry Moore hosted a popular show called "I've Got a Secret" wherein a panel of four celebrities tried to guess a guest's possession, occupation, unique event, hobby, or achievement. Many times the panel could gain an advantage and solve the career challenge if they asked good questions.

Similarly, pickleball players can gain an advantage if they learn to use basic elements of geometry during their games. Here is the basic principle (and the corollaries will follow):

A fundamental principle.
If you hit the ball straight toward your opponent's forehand side, it is relatively easy for him/her to hit it back to you. The associated principle of this is: The *harder* you hit the ball straight at your opponent, (in general) they *faster* it will be returned to you. In short, the use of power is somewhat overrated for use in pickleball.

Create angled shots.
Once you know and accept (internalize) the basic principle, it then makes sense to use it to your advantage by *changing the direction of your strokes*. The fundamental corollary of the basic principle can then be stated thus: *Change the angle of your shots as much as possible, and this will often result in winners for two reasons—it will be more difficult for your opponent to hit a shot that is angled, and also an angled shot will be more likely to catch the opponent by surprise.* This is true of dinks, volleys, smashes, and groundstrokes. In effect, angled shots work to your advantage, so try to use them!

For example, if you are dinking straight across both non-volley zones, the distance is 14 feet. However, if you are dinking from one extreme corner of your NVZ to the extreme corner of the opponent's NVZ, the distance is about 24.5 feet—a space that is over 50% longer. If you are serving the ball, the shortest distance (virtually right down the center line) is slightly longer than 44 feet.

However, if you serve from your own far corner to the opponent's far corner, the distance available to you is over 48 feet. A successful corner-to-corner serve (holding other factors constant) therefore drives your opponent back a considerable distance and makes it more difficult for him/her to get to the NVZ line after returning your serve. At a minimum, it helps to open up the middle for a return shot.

Another analysis of angles comes into play during the initial return of serve and resultant third shot *drive* options (holding aside the possibility of a third shot drop). Since most recreational players will attempt to return the serve with their forehand, the targets for the returner might include the server's forehand side (not recommended), the server's backhand side, the partner's forehand side (not recommended), and the partner's backhand side. The returner, therefore, has two "good" target areas at which to aim.

Any returner's shot delivered accidentally or intentionally to the server's forehand side gives the server four good options: 1) a line drive down the sideline (hoping to catch the returner's partner off guard on the backhand side), 2) a lob over the returner's partner (also a surprise offensive shot), 3) a middle drive straight to the returner's backhand as the returner moves up toward the NVZ, or 4) a more sharply *angled* shot to the returner's forehand side while the returner is moving toward the NVZ.

Conclusion.

As you develop from a Beginner to an Intermediate level player you should always be thinking of *aiming* and *angling* your shots toward a specific target (instead of simply attempting to get the ball back over the net). Ask yourself these questions: *"What's my target?"* and *"What's my angle?"* and you will improve your chances of success.

CHAPTER 6

Attitude & Strategy on the Court

CHOOSING AND USING A PMA

Positive Mental Attitude (PMA)—what is it?
Developed cooperatively many years ago in a book by Napoleon Hill and W. Clement Stone, a positive mental attitude (PMA) is an *optimistic state of mind that seeks ways to win or obtain a positive outcome even under difficult circumstances.* People with a PMA (which might include the surviving prisoners of war from the Viet Nam conflict) often demonstrate the characteristics of hope, courage, initiative, kindliness, and integrity.

Negative Mental Attitude (NMA)—what is it?
The opposite characteristics of a PMA might include negativity, defeatism, and hopelessness. When you hear yourself making negative comments on the court such as "They're just too good for us" or "Should we even ask them for another game?" or "I just can't hit that shot" (or worse—cursing regularly) while playing pickleball, that is a strong indication that you have a negative mental attitude. Unfortunately, a negative attitude often becomes a self-fulfilling prophecy; because your attitude is bad you then make bad shots and then your attitude deteriorates even further as a result of the continuing self-critique that you engage in.

How can you develop a PMA in pickleball?
1. Find a good instructor/mentor and practice your astute listening skills and open mind so as to maximize your learning from that individual.
2. Choose to play pickleball most often with upbeat individuals—those people who are capable of laughing at their own foibles, and who typically uplift others around them.
3. Keep looking for something new to stimulate your brain. Try serving backhanded, or attempt an "around the post" shot. Watch a few pickleball videos on YouTube.
4. Realize that pickleball (like life itself) has both ups and downs. Almost everyone has a single "bad hair day" occasionally, but subsequent days or games can often be

better. Did you make a bad shot? A series of mistakes? Put them behind you and move on! Focus your energies and concentrate on the *next* shot.

5. Commit yourself at the start of a game to focus on *one thing*, such as serving to your opponent's backhand, or improving your dinking game, or making offensive lobs. Big progress can come from successful little improvements in your game. Give yourself credit when things go well or improve.

6. Seek out and talk to other players, or develop a relationship with informal pickleball coaches. Ask them to provide you with constructive feedback and bits of advice (along with praise).

Conclusion.

Playing pickleball should be fun. *Make it so* for yourself and others by committing yourself to exhibit a positive mental attitude!

SUCCESS COMES IN CANS, NOT CANNOTS!*

In a separate item (see the previous "Choosing and Using a PMA"), I've written about the value of having (in life, and in pickleball) a *Positive Mental Attitude*. Nevertheless, I regularly hear (or see, in the facial expressions of self-doubters) the stubborn phrase of "I can't." Because of this attitude, the person resists trying a new way to improve (often through asserting "But..." or stating that "I've tried that before and it didn't work") and this makes it extremely difficult for an instructor or coach to help them. As a former colleague of mine famously (but sorrowfully) said, "You can't push a rope."

Fifty years ago, when we first saw a person with a disability, it was often assumed that individual was unable to perform a work task or athletic feat. We may have concluded that ("They can't."). Unfortunately, we not only tell ourselves that "*We* can't," we often tell others that *they* can't, either! In effect, we impose arbitrary limitations on ourselves and on others. Fortunately, we've now learned that they not only *can* do what we previously thought impossible, they can often do amazingly *well* at it. If you think about it, there admittedly *are* a few things we can't do, but (fortunately) there are many things we *can* control and *can* do.

What CAN'T you do ("Cannots") on the pickleball court? Examples include:
- You can't make yourself any younger.
- You can't control your opponent's skill level.
- You can't control the weather conditions (heat, rain, wind).
- You can't change the last shot you made.

What CAN you do? Illustrations include:
- You *can* learn new skills.
- You *can* improve your fitness level.
- You *can* learn new pickleball strategies.
- You *can* practice (even alone, or at home).
- You *can* be a better team player/partner.

- You *can* communicate more.
- You *can* focus on the next point/next shot.
- You *can* mentally shut out distractions.
- You *can* orally support your partner.
- You *can* focus on better shot selection.
- You *can* develop a high success rate on your serves.
- You *can* choose to hydrate yourself before, during, and after a game.
- You *can* help your partner enjoy the current game.
- You *can* focus all your mental and physical energy on self-improvement.
- You *can* change your team's strategy during a game (in a time out).

Conclusion:

Place your greatest focus of attention on your "Cans," and refuse to be seduced into thinking only of your "Cannots."

*I've borrowed this phrase from superstar speaker Joel Weldon.

"BOOKMAKING" AND THE COMPLETE PICKLEBALLER

Classic examples.
In the terminology of gamblers, *bookmaking* is "the practice of determining the odds and receiving and paying off bets on the various possible outcomes of a single event" (e.g., in horse racing, political contests, or athletic competitions). Historically, these wagers were recorded in a private hard-bound ledger, and collectively used to adjust the odds on the event so as to allow the bookmaker ("bookie") to usually come out ahead after paying off the winners. (Some of this bookmaking was done illegally, however.)

In the world of sports, coaches and players are always on the lookout for an "edge"—information that will give them a winning advantage. They scout the opposition, identify their tactics and patterns, and map out a plan (make a playbook) to follow. The wildly popular book and movie, *"Moneyball,"* exemplified this approach in the world of baseball, documenting the success (through data gathering and data analysis) of the Oakland Athletics and its general manager, Billy Beane.

In the for-profit domain, organizations have increasingly used *business analytics* (large amounts of data that are statistically analyzed and converted into algorithms to aid in fact-based decision-making). This process consists of skills, technologies, and practices to gain insight and improve business planning (in an attempt to gain a legitimate and useful edge).

Pickleball bookmaking.
In pickleball, nationally famous "Coach Mo" (Richard Movsessian) advises his students to engage in an ethical form of bookmaking. He suggests that a player make mental notes on each opponent that is faced on a regular basis and then record these systematically in a notebook. These notes might include observations and private comments on an opponent's strengths, tendencies, weaknesses, and types of errors commonly made. In effect, he argues that you should "get to know your opponents" by making a book and using that information to your advantage.

An abbreviated version of such a book for pickleballers might take the form of a matrix that lists frequent (or upcoming opponents' names on one axis, and a set of common weaknesses of behaviors on the other axis. These latter factors, for example might include behaviors such as:

- Has a weak backhand
- Often makes short serves
- Stays primarily at the baseline
- Dislikes the dinking game
- Has a poor third shot drop
- Is a southpaw (left handed)
- Never chases down a lob
- Lacks sideways mobility
- Gets frustrated easily
- Makes frequent foot faults at the NVZ line
- Is capable of making the Erne shot
- Has a hard, low, deep serve
- Often leaves the middle unprotected

In summary, to paraphrase a popular "Capital One" credit card commercial that asks viewers, "What's in *your* wallet?" might instead ask you, "What's in *your* book? The answer, i detailed and accurate, just might give you an extra edge over the opponents in your next game. You now have a new job description—that of "bookie."

CHARACTER COUNTS ON THE PB COURT

Character tripled.

John DeFilippo was hired as the Offensive Coordinator for the Minnesota Vikings football team. One of his first tasks was to help select the starting quarterback for the team. What did he look for in that quarterback (who turned out to be Kirk Cousins)? *"Character, character, character"* was his immediate response. To expand on that, DeFilippo said the quarterback must love the game, set a good example, and get along with his teammates. An essential element that is notable in successful quarterbacks is one's *visible physical demeanor;* good body language demands exhibiting it so others will see it, interpret it both properly and positively, and act appropriately themselves. In short, a positive demeanor (character) is "catchy" and spreads to others.

What does this have to do with pickleball? Quite a bit, I believe. Just as a bad apple can begin to spoil a whole barrel of them, so can a negative person impact his/her partners (and opponents). Here are a couple of examples from where I play in Florida. I participate in two local PB groups, numbering about 60 people in total. The vast majority of them (i.e., 97%) are not only solid players but also genuinely positive individuals who support each other's efforts and enjoy playing the game.

Examples of poor character.

Two persons, however, stand out for their negative attitudes such that several players even refuse to play with them. Why? Because any time that I (or anyone else who is their partner) make a mistake or hit a poor shot (a UFER), their facial expression, eyeball rolling, and body language immediately and powerfully conveys a message of deep disappointment and dismay. The ripple effect of this is to lower their partner's pickleball-related self-esteem and this soon leads to even *more* mistakes because of the feeling of being negatively and harshly and unfairly judged on a constant basis. The result—whether a win or a loss ensues—is that neither I nor my other pickleball colleagues enjoy that particular game (and sometimes it even affects subsequent games that day). Pickleball should be, and can be, *fun* for its participants!

I, too, need to be watchful and introspective about my *own* behavior. Here is an example: frequently I find myself (in another area of the country) partnering (because of rotating from the sidelines into the next foursomes) with a fellow who can charitably be described as a "klutz" on the court—and one who has shown no interest in self-improvement over time. I need to be extremely careful not to "wear my heart on my sleeve" and display my internal feelings via my body posture or facial expressions (or critical verbal remarks!) when playing with him. This, admittedly, is not easy for me. However, I need to view it as an opportunity to demonstrate a little bit of what Vikings coach DeFilippo demands—*character*.

Bottom line:

To my great pleasure (and relief), I have never yet encountered a PB player in my local playing area who exhibits the negative body language described above. Maybe this is an indirect demonstration of the legendary *"Minnesota Nice"* characteristic that has been much discussed in the popular press? Regardless of its source, I sincerely hope that "character on the court" continues to exhibit itself in *your* life and in mine!

Illustrations of good character.

Here are a few other ways to make your good character count on the court: smile, use appropriate humor, avoid profanity, *toss* the ball (after a point is over) to your opponent, avoid making "out" calls on the other court, make generous line calls on your side of the court, respect the rotation system at your court, call your own violations (e.g., foot faults), and be complimentary to others. You may be amazed at the response!

CONTROLLING THE "CONTROLLABLES"

The value of failure.
A recent issue of the *Minneapolis StarTrib* had a nice article on "Why losing at sports can be good." Although directed at high school kids, I still found Eliza McGraw's comments useful for pickleballers. She pointed out that most of us lose (or win) about 50% of the time, yet we can learn important lessons from failure (e.g., camaraderie, sportsmanship, humility, and the value of incremental change).

Multiple variables.
Success in competition not only depends on one's own talent and developed skill, but also the skill of your opponents, the accuracy of the referees, the weather conditions (e.g., wind and rain), bad luck (e.g., a bad lie of the ball in golf), and other factors. Should we then simply throw up our hands and capitulate when things don't go our way? Not necessarily! In short, there are many variables (*"controllables"*) under our auspices.

I believe that we can "control the controllables" if we just identify and focus on them. In pickleball, there are numerous items that are *exclusively* under our control both before and during a game—no matter how talented our opponents might be. What are they? Here is a short list of some items:

1. *Paddle position.* I can *always* hold my paddle at waist or chest-high level. This both prepares me for returning a sharp volley at the NVZ line, as well as helps me protect my face from a painful shot received.

2. *Court position.* I can place myself in the right position (forward, back, left, right, and out of "No man's land")—at least at the beginning of a point.

3. *Hydration.* I can drink liquid in advance of playing, between games, and even during games to prevent foot and leg cramps (or fainting).

4. *Serving.* Even if I am facing the world's best pickleball player, I can still achieve my goal of getting 100% of my serves in the proper box. This requires both practice and concentration, of course.

5. *Stretching.* I can stretch my back, my arms, and my legs to loosen them up every time *before* I begin play. This may prevent some injuries.

6. *Risk taking.* I can make good decisions about whether to take unnecessary chances at difficult balls. I can vow never to backpedal to return a lob. I can *prepare* my body, and *listen* to my body.

7. *Attitude.* I can choose be positive about myself, my opponents, and the game I'm playing (a PMA), or I can let my (negative) thoughts distract me and affect my play.

8. *Teamwork.* I can choose to view myself as the star of the team, or I can give my partner a chance to demonstrate and grow his/her skills.

9. *Communication.* I can send messages to my partner on nearly every shot (e.g., "Mine," or "Yours" or "I'll take it" or "Let it go").

10. *Play the percentages.* I can choose to hit high-probability shots (e.g., "Down the middle") instead of taking chances by aiming just inside the lines.

11. *Watch the ball.* I can focus closely on the ball the instant it leaves my opponent's paddle, and then track its movement until it hits my own paddle.

12. *Watch prospective opponents.* I can use my spare (sideline) time to observe and mentally note the strengths, weaknesses, and general tendencies of my impending opponents (see "Bookmaking").

Those are just 12 things that I have near-total control over even before I step onto the court. Now…*will you do them*? Promise yourself you will *control the controllables.*

THE IMPORTANCE OF "ONE"

I was reflecting recently on the significance of the word "**one**." Obviously, I've barely scratched the surface of its relevance in many domains, but a few citations quickly came to mind (in philosophy, songs, plays, and sports). For example:

• "The journey of a thousand miles begins with a single (**one**) step." (Lao Tzu)

• "**One** is the loneliest number…" (song written by Harry Nilsson and recorded famously by Three Dog Night)

• "**One**" singular sensation…**one** thrilling combination…**one** smile…**one** of a kind (from the musical *Chorus Line*)

• "Just **one** voice singing in the darkness, all it takes is **one** voice…and every**one** will sing!" (Barry Manilow)

• The Univ. of Minnesota Duluth hockey team earned its way into the 2018 NCAA "Frozen Four" tournament against all odds by the tiniest fraction—**one** *ten thousandth of a point* (and the team subsequently won each of its games on the road to the national Division I championship by **one** goal).

The importance of the number "**one**" is also embedded in my experiences with pickleball—and *not* because I ever have any dreams of being "#1." Far from it! Here are some thoughts that have emerged in my mental wanderings:

• I regularly see pickleball players at every skill level fail to make a successful serve on occasion—the simplest of all strokes. This potentially costs their team a minimum of **one** point, and possibly as many as the next *ten* points as well.

• I see (and hear) egotistical players acting as if they are the most important person on their team—the **one** who is better than the other. This often results in an uncoordinated set of two persons acting independently rather than as **one** integrated team who communicate well and display complementary skills. Long-time winning PB teams (e.g., Jennifer Lucore and Alex Hamner) play and move and think as **one**.

• Every PB coach that I have observed or listened to (e.g., "Coach Mo," or Robert Elliott, or Deb Harrison) preaches the importance of *minimizing unforced errors and mental mistakes.* Again, I often observe (and unfortunately exhibit myself) how **one** single error (i.e., a muffed return of serve, or a risky-but-wide shot, or a missed lob, or a foot fault) can turn a winning game into a losing outcome. *Play high-percentage PB!*

• A pickleball partner and I were losing badly (e.g., 9-2) in a recent game when he (jokingly?) said to me "Maybe we should already start asking our opponents for a rematch." This brought to mind my all-time favorite pickleball experience—a game in which my partner that day (Len Hathaway) and I were down 10-0 to a pair of skilled opponents. He and I conferred briefly, and agreed that we needed to win at least **one** point to avoid the embarrassment of a complete shutout (e.g., being "pickled"). (As I recall, I quoted the famous WWII rallying cry of Winston Churchill, who urged English citizens on October 29, 1941 to "Never give in, never give in, never, never, never, never—in nothing…"). Thus refocused, my partner and I won the next rally for **one** point, and then won a second **one**, and then another, until after winning twelve straight points we finally defeated our opponents by a score of 12-10! That experience vividly illustrated to me the importance of **one** point (each point). It does little good to berate yourself for the *last* point lost; it does more good to commit yourself to doing your best to win at least **one** more point—the *next* **one**.

Yes, I believe that the number "**one**" is important in pickleball!

PICKLEBALL ANTICIPATION

During a recent pickleball game my partner made what I considered to be a very good shot and I commended him for it. He responded, "It was pure instinct." I doubted that explanation, as an instinctive behavior is one that is biologically innate or inherent (not based on prior experience). Instinct is *not* learned.

An alternative to instinct

I suspect that the player actually might have meant (or intended to say) that he was simply *reacting* to a momentary stimulus (the ball), but that interpretation is not very fruitful for responding to future challenges. Another, more viable, possibility is that he had actually practiced the art of *anticipation*, in which a player cognitively (if momentarily) considers and computes the likelihood of an expected event and then acts appropriately.

What, then, constitutes *anticipation*? Singer Carly Simon once crooned (in the song by that title) "We can never know about the days to come, but we *think* about them anyway." According to *Dictionary.com,* anticipation involves forward-looking contemplation and forethought. It is based on readiness, wherein someone has presupposed or expected a future event *and prepared for its prospect.* (The military, not surprisingly, has an alliterative slogan for this practice, summarized variously as the "7 Ps". The all-purpose version suggests that "Proper Planning and Preparation Prevents P***-Poor Performance.") Interestingly, anticipation is often associated (in one's personal life) with negative emotions such as misgivings, forebodings, apprehensiveness, and even alarm, but it can also connote feelings of excitement or pleasure that lie ahead.

Ways to use anticipation

On the pickleball court, good players use anticipation to shift the odds of success in their favor through preparedness. Here are some ways in which pickleball anticipation might operate:

1. An anticipatory player consults his/her "book" (see "Bookmaking" in Chapter 6) on an opponent to determine and respond to that person's common tendencies (e.g., if

the opponent typically attempts to serve to the backhand side).

2. An anticipatory player focuses on an opponent's eyes to make predictions about which direction he or she will drive the ball (just as a defensive back in football watches a quarterback's eyes to see where he will throw a pass).

3. An anticipatory player takes note regarding where on the court the opponent (and ball) is, and then either moves over to protect against a down-the-line shot or else shifts slightly toward the middle to cover a shot down that channel.

When is pickleball anticipation dysfunctional?

As useful as anticipation can be, it can also have a "down" side to it. For example, a player may *overthink* a situation and then not be able to react as quickly as otherwise required. Another illustration occurs when a player anticipates that an opponent will "float" a shot cross-court to one's partner and hence attempts to execute a poach. If this player then finds out that the opponent has made a different shot (e.g., a lob or a drive down the sideline), the tactic will have backfired.

Conclusion

For over 100 years, the motto of the Boy Scouts, Girl Guides, and Girl Scouts has urged its members to "Be Prepared." The principle is explained to youth through an emphasis on both *mind* (advance mental preparedness to know and do the right thing) and *body* (being physically active and strong enough to act accordingly). The Scout motto is highly relevant to pickleballers, who can study and draw upon an emerging body of knowledge about *how* to play well and combine it with their own personalized practice of *anticipation* to result in improved play over time.

Note: For those players interested in their own self-assessment and improvement, the rating criteria for a 3.5 player includes this statement—(These players) are learning to *anticipate* opponents' shots."

IMPROVING PROBABLE PERFORMANCE

Question:

> *What major (individual) factors influence or affect one's long-term performance (success) on the pickleball court* (holding aside both environmental conditions and your opponents' skill levels)?

Response (simplified):

There are three major underlying considerations (the "three As"), as follows:

1.   *Agility (A^1)*—athleticism/nimbleness, or the ability to move quickly and easily;
2.   *Attitude (A^2)*—the positive or negative propensity one has to respond in a characteristic way; the desire to learn/grow/improve by discovering new ways to behave via coaching and feedback;
3.   *Analysis (A^3)*—the intellectual ability to do mental calculations of angles and probabilities, embrace tactical/strategic suggestions, and incorporate these into flexible on-the-court play.

A Formula.

These three broad factors can be combined multiplicatively to produce *Probable Performance (PP)*, such that

$$A^1 \times A^2 \times A^3 = PP$$

The immediate implication of this "formula for success" is that it takes at least a modest degree of *all three factors* to create an overall (sustained) high performance level. Further, if any one factor is totally lacking, the chance for ongoing success is virtually absent.

Implication:

Rate yourself on all three factors on a mythical scale from 0 (low) to 10 (high). Then multiply those numbers together to produce your own Probable Performance index (hint: divide your answer by 100 to again produce a 0-10 index). Now consider which of those factors (1, 2, or all 3) is most *susceptible* to change. How *much* change is possible for you? Where is *your* greatest *opportunity* for improvement on the pickleball court likely to come from?

The Role of Coaching:
    I suggest that, at least in the short term, a pickleball friend/coach can't do much to improve another player's natural or current *athleticism* (other than to suggest a series of agility and/or conditioning drills). It is difficult for a coach to turn around a player's *attitude* toward learning in a few hours of time; that is largely an internal decision by the player (but can be certainly be *assisted* by a counselor or friend). There are numerous things that a pickleball coach *can* do to improve a player's *knowledge and skill,* however, such that the A^3 factor takes a substantial leap forward (under sustained practice). These roles include (but are not limited to) the following:

1. *Close observation* of the player's strengths and weaknesses (sometimes supplemented by photographic or video evidence), followed by personalized feedback and individualized goal-setting.
2. *Use of numerous drills* to provide focused practice and repetition (i.e., on serving, returning the serve, dinking, lobbing, volleying, and the infamous "third shot drop"). As Aristotle reportedly said, "We are what we repeatedly do."
3. *Discussion of elements* such as court position, body posture, paddle position, footwork, partner communication, court geometry (angles), shot probabilities, poaching, "Churchill's Law," re-setting the point from defense to offense, choosing targets, keeping a "book" on opponents, and playing percentage pickleball (minimizing unforced errors).

THE "SEVEN P'S" OF PICKLEBALL

It is sometimes easier to remember the key points of what to know and do if you have a memory aid to help you focus your efforts as you approach each point and each game. Here are seven important elements (the alliterative "Seven P's) that might contribute to your success and enjoyment of this great game:

1. *Position* (standing in the correct place to begin a point; moving your feet to be in the best place to return a shot; staying out of "No Man's Land"). Predictably, some beginner players feel reluctant to advance (after the return of serve) all the way up to the NVZ line; they park themselves about 4 feet or more behind it and often stay in that position. Consequently they get caught with the opponent's shot hitting at their feet in "No Man's Land." Another difficulty occurs when a player (i.e., the partner of the server) either takes a position in front of the baseline during the serve or immediately edges forward a step or two and then gets caught mistakenly forgetting the "Double Bounce" rule. "Stay back until the serve is returned" will prevent this error. Try standing on the baseline while your partner serves, and watch his/her feet for possible foot faults.

2. *Placement.* The simplest and usually the safest and most effective target for your shots is between your opponents (the "*Golden Middle*"). Accuracy of ball placement is worth striving for, as it reduces the number of errors you make.

3. *Practice.* This means seriously working on the weakest element of your repertoire *before* you start to play each day, and repetition of new skills (with guided coaching and constructive feedback). FYI, my golf coach recently advised that I needed to make *2000* repetitions of my coach-advised swing before it would become natural for me to do it.

4. *Patience.* Don't try for a "winner" every time you hit a shot. Use the law of probability (e.g., How successful have you been in the past when you've hit that shot?)

and only rarely hit a shot that doesn't have a reasonably good chance of success. Practice multiple dinks, or try matching an opponent groundstroke for groundstroke until you have a clear opportunity to hit a probable winner.

5. ***Power.*** This is most appropriately done when you hit an overhead smash. Even then, most pros suggest hitting with only about 80% of your potential power in order to minimize the chance of hitting the ball out of bounds (too long) or prematurely (into the net).

6. ***Poaching.*** A highly effective tactic to catch the opponents off guard is to make a sudden surprise move (usually from the left court to the right court) to cut of a ground stroke or soft "lift" that your opponent is trying to hit to your partner who may still be several feet behind the NVZ (for example, after the return of serve). This creates a quicker and faster return of the ball than expected, and often catches the server and/or server's partner unprepared as they are still in the process of moving toward the NVZ line on their side of the court. Unpredictability is the key here; try not to "telegraph" your move.

7. ***Praise.*** Support and encourage your partners and opponents with positive and focused oral comments!

COMMON WAYS TO *LOSE* POINTS

Top pickleball players and coaches explain that most points are not *won* through brilliant and skillful shots by the superior team. Instead, they are *lost* due to mistakes and unforced errors on the part of the other team. Some of these errors are mental, and some are physical, reminding us that it is critical to keep both your mind and body prepared and involved in the game at all times.

The vast majority of points lost come about due to these types of mistakes. *Don't make them* (repeatedly)!

1. Failing to "keep your paddle up" at all times to be prepared for an opponent's shot.
2. Not making powerful, assertive shots deep into the opponents' court so as to keep them buried at their baseline.
3. Not "side-stepping" in concert with your partner's movement on the court (i.e., maintaining the "eight foot rope" idea).
4. Failing to move your feet for repositioning between shots.
5. Failing to aim your torso and lead shoulder toward your target.
6. Failing to switch sides when your partner goes back for a lob behind you.
7. "Lifting" your shots and thus allowing your opponents to easily smash the ball at your feet (or your partner's feet).
8. Not positioning yourself properly on the court at the start of a new point (three players back, one up at the NVZ line).
9. Not remembering the 'two-bounce" rule.
10. Missing your serve (i.e., not being 95-100% accurate).
11. Not noticing or adapting to the direction and strength of the wind.
12. Assuming that a great shot you made will not be returned by your opponent.
13. Attempting to hit winning shots from below the level of the net.

14. Serving (or receiving the serve) from the wrong position on the court.
15. Trying to hit a winner on every shot (impatience).

POSSIBLE PICKLEBALL PLAYER RESOLUTIONS: A CHECKLIST

There are literally dozens of "prescriptions" for pickleball success, and each player has the option of choosing which ones to focus on for his/her own success. By way of summary, here are 44 optional resolutions to consider. "I intend to:

1. Keep my paddle up at all times during the course of a point.
2. Consciously choose a position on the court to optimize coverage.
3. Cover for my partner who has moved off the court during play.
4. Stay out of "No Man's Land".
5. Communicate with my partner re: "Who protects the middle?"
6. Strive to be 100% successful with my serves.
7. Attempt to hit my serves deep or to the backhand side.
8. Develop and utilize a "book" on my typical opponents.
9. Position my feet and body so as to be ready to move at all times.
10. Modify the pace of my shots from fast/hard to slow/soft.
11. Become more well-rounded so that I am comfortable with my forehand, backhand, smashes, pushes, and dinks.
12. Make my returns of serve either soft and deep, or to my opponent's backhand side.
13. Get to the net immediately following my return of serve.
14. Never hit the third shot until the second bounce has occurred.
15. Watch the ball all the way until it contacts my paddle (rather than looking at my target).
16. Always stretch and warm up prior to playing.
17. Remember to loudly yell "Ball on Court!" when a ball goes astray.
18. Consider joining the USAPA (see: usapa.org).
19. Square my body to my opponent who will hit the ball.
20. Aim my lead shoulder toward my opponent when hitting forehand or backhand shots.

21. Commit to executing a planned or spontaneous poach on appropriate occasions.
22. Never, ever run backwards to hit a ball.
23. Never call a ball "in" or "out" on my opponent's court unless asked.
24. Remember that a ball hit hard to my opponent will likely return to me even faster.
25. Give the benefit of the doubt to my opponents when there are close line calls.
26. Strive for control and consistency over the use of power.
27. Practice hitting shots aimed at the "Golden Middle."
28. Move my feet while in a dinking battle.
29. Aim my lobs at my opponent's backhand side.
30. Actively use my left hand and arm to aim my lead shoulder and balance my body.
31. Imagine that I am hitting 3-4 balls consecutively when driving the ball.
32. Use the wind (and sun) to my advantage.
33. Never switch hands unless I am truly ambidextrous.
34. Use my knowledge of angles to my advantage.
35. Use mostly a snap of my wrist when hitting smashes/slams.
36. Consider hitting serves and shots to the longest point of the court (the corners).
37. Aim my dinks at a "window" that is at least 6" over the net.
38. "Lean in" to shorten the Non Volley Zone; take some shots in the air.
39. Use a soft grip and minimal backswing on dinks and third shot drops.
40. Maximize shots that (through repetition) have a high likelihood of success.
41. Monitor my facial expression, body language, and utterances so as not to irritate or discourage my partner.
42. Play to win, but be a gracious loser.
43. Never relax until the point is clearly over ("Churchill's Law").
45. Follow the USAPA's Code of Conduct.

CHAPTER 7

Frivolous Items

TWENTY SIGNS OF PICKLEBALL ADDICTION

Definition of addiction:

It is the compulsive and repetitive (and often unthinking) engagement of a behavior. The addictive behavior is self-perceived as being inherently positive, desirable, and pleasurable (although it might no be to an objective observer). Some players enjoy pickleball so much that they, too, could be considered as "addicts." You might be a *pickleball (PB) addict* if you:

1. Dream about pickleball at night.
2. Play pickleball more than 3 times per week.
3. Will drop all other planned activities to play pickleball when asked.
4. Use the phrase "Just one more game" several times in one day.
5. Claim that you "just play for fun," but always play to win.
6. Continually search for the best new paddle to improve your game.
7. Wear "I Love Pickleball" shirts everywhere you go.
8. Watch YouTube clips about pickleball for hours on end during rainy days.
9. Engage guests with tales of your latest attempts to master the "third shot drop."
10. List an 11-0 pickleball victory among your life's greatest achievements.
11. Include "Pickleball Addict" in the rough draft of your obituary.
12. Love to help other players improve their pickleball skills.
13. Regale your friends about every injury and pulled muscle you've ever incurred while playing pickleball.
14. Keep a secret notebook with info on the weaknesses of your opponents.
15. Sport a pickleball-related bumper sticker on your car.
16. Look up "Places to Play Pickleball" as you plan your vacation trips.

17. Think it's almost never too hot, too cold, or too windy to play pickleball.
18. Immediately bounce up and say "I'm OK!" after taking a hard fall.
19. Start every conversation with newly-met friends by asking "Have you ever played pickleball?"
20. Eat, sleep, and breathe pickleball 24/7.

THE "OH OH" SHOT: NEGATING THE PERFECT LOB

Background

A previous item focused on *the lob shot*—a deeply lofted shot usually hit off a bounce that is intended to land behind your opponent and be difficult (if not impossible) to return. That essay differentiated between an offensive lob and a defensive lob, and also described three main tactics to use when an opponent lobs over your head.

Some players have developed not only excellent skill at lobbing, but also at disguising their *intent* to lob and their actual stroke. This can often be embarrassing to the team that is caught off guard when a lob goes over their head and is unreachable.

A Perfect Solution

Fortunately, someone has engaged in an extensive and careful study of ancient lore hidden deep in the archives of the National Pickleball Library in Washington, D.C. This investigation uncovered the existence of a little-known tactic for the ideal defense against a surprise lob. Named by its inventor, "Mr. X" (a modest person who humbly wishes to remain anonymous), the tactic is a brilliantly simple one. According to the legend uncovered by "Mr. X," either member of the defensive team (when facing a lob) need merely to utter aloud the two words **"Oh, Oh!"** *while the ball is in the air*. (It is too late to use this tactic after the ball strikes the court.)

The **"Oh Oh"** pronouncement represents a formal and public praise for the beauty and elegance of the lob along with a submissively grudging acknowledgment of the defensive inadequacy of the recipient team. (In effect, it is basically a desperate plea to the other team to *not count* [e.g., to negate or invalidate] the effect of the lob.) Admittedly, it takes a great deal of humility to make this admission, but that is certainly a small price to pay for the benefit received.

The Result

It is widely believed that a humane and sympathetic lobbing team will then rest on their laurels from knowing that they *could* have scored a point, and they will thereby sympathetically and voluntarily negate the point. In effect (in their minds), the lobbing team will have scored *two* points—one for the effective lob, and one for crushing the very souls of the receiving team and forcing them to admit their lack of defensive skill. This, then, is truly a win-win situation, whereby the defending team escapes having a point scored against them for the inexpensive price of using two simple words.

The Need for Advance Practice

This **"Oh Oh"** shot is a tactic that an aspiring pickleballer can practice at home or in the car. Simply repeat (aloud) the words **"Oh, Oh!"** until it comes naturally and it instantaneously rolls off your lips. (Note: it might help if you inform your opponents in advance regarding your intention to invoke this well-hidden rule, or else you might encounter some resistance to its spontaneous use.

Trust me; this "Oh Oh!" shot will inevitably come in handy some day!

THE "BENDA" SHOT

Headline:

According to local (Aitkin) legend, the United States of America Pickleball Association (USAPA) board of directors has recently voted to recognize and endorse the "Benda" shot. They may even include a description of it in their official Rulebook at some point in the future. Members of the Aitkin Area Pickleball Association were elated to hear about this honor bestowed upon one of their own members—"Gentleman Jim" Benda.

Background:

Jim, who apparently has a strong (self-taught) background in Euclidean geometry and the physics/trajectories of moving objects, studied at length the ideal height of a pickleball shot (hard groundstroke) made from the baseline. As a consequence, he determined that the perfect shot moved at a slight upward angle as it crossed just over the net and had a ground speed of exactly 32 mph. (Repeated additional height and speed resulted in rapid tiring of the person who fired the projectile.) He subsequently discovered that skilled opponents such as those he regularly encountered on the court could soon adapt to the "bullet-like" shots of "bangers" and return those shots with ease.

That is when he had an epiphany or "Aha!" moment (much like Archimedes did, when he first coined the phrase "Eureka, I have found it!"). By lowering his aim approximately 1 5/16th of an inch, he found that his ball would strike the strip at the top of the net and thus create confusion in his opponent. After literally hundreds of hours of extremely deep thought, extensive study, and painstaking experimentation, he went on to identify and refine *three* distinctive "Benda" shots, which he initially (and humbly) labeled as Type A, Type B, and Type C. Soon, however, his many admirers on the court felt that the typology did not provide Jim with enough credit, and so they applied more sophisticated descriptive labels to the three "Benda" shots, as follows:

Type A (the "*Bare Bones Benda*")—This shot hits the top of the net and immediately drops on the other side, causing great distress to any opponent who has either stayed too far back from the NVZ line, or does not have lightning-quick reflexes.

Type B (the "*Body Blow Benda*")—This shot hits a little less of the net's top edge, and thus its trajectory is suddenly distorted upward into a new path that catches the opponent off guard as it strikes his/her body. The result is that (no matter how well prepared the opponent is for an *honest and fair* shot), the ball is usually non-returnable (and a blow to the recipient's ego).

Type C ("the *Befuddling Benda*")—This shot hits the tape at the top of the net almost squarely, and the unbelievable top spin *and side spin* applied are sufficient to make the ball roll along the top of the net for one or two feet before dropping safely on the opponent's side of the net (thus befuddling them).

The Benda Effect:

Not only does Jim and his lucky partner usually win a point (or prevent the opponent from scoring), but also he and his partner only need approximately two Benda shots in one game to totally demoralize the opposing team (the cumulative "Benda Effect").

Defending the Benda:

There is currently no known "cure" or antidote for the Benda Effect on others.

PICKLEBALL CLICHES

Definition of cliché:
      A cliché is a trite (but memorable) expression that, although it conveys an idea or principle, may become overused or discounted as simply "cute." Nevertheless, clichés may come in handy as a way to tease an opponent or to make a seemingly constructive comment to your partner. Here is a sampling of overheard pickleball-oriented clichés:

"To improve your skills, you gotta do the drills."
"Practice with a purpose."
"Down the middle solves the riddle."
"Serve it deep, to make them weep."
"Practice like you've never won; perform like you've never lost."
"If well they can't play, then make them pay."
"Hit a good lob, and they will sob."
"Use your best dink to make them think."
"Hit a hard smash, & they'll say *Alas!*"
"Hit a high service, and they'll be nervous."
"When you crisply return their serve, it'll soon break their nerve."
"If the ball is 'out', say it with a shout."
"Hit a great volley, and you'll be jolly."
"With a third shot drop, you'll come out on top."
"It's never shoddy to protect your body."
"If they fling their paddle, it's best to skedaddle."
"If your knuckles are white, you're holding it too tight."
"Your shots will be bolder if you lead with your shoulder."
"Increase your talents when you focus on balance."
"Aim for the scarlet on your opponent's chest target."
"Keep your nose out over your toes."
"Your opponents will bend when you play points to the end."
"If from the line you oft retreat, you'll soon wind up in a big defeat."
"Hold tight to the line, and you'll do just fine."
"Aim your shots at the toes of your opponents and foes."
"If you hit as you run, the point soon will be done."
"If the ball is too tall, back up and you'll fall."

"When in doubt, don't call it out."

"If you want your groundstroke to go, keep your body really low."

"To raise your game and make it tower, focus on placement instead of power."

"Your return of serve needs to be fine, to give you time to get to the line."

"If too oft you miss your serve, soon you'll find you've lost your nerve."

"If you want pickleball fame, then your shots you should aim."

"Practice as you will play, and you will play as you practiced."

"If the winning shot you can't now take, *reset the point* for goodness' sake!"

A PICKLEBALL LAMENT

There is something about the Pickleball game,
That makes playing it rather pleasant;
But as I volley, and dink, and lob,
I wish my skills were more present.

There is something about the Pickleball game,
That stimulates my mind and my hunger;
My only regret as I consider my age,
I wish that I were much younger!

There is something about the Pickleball game,
That intrigues me more than a little;
Why can't I get it through my head,
To hit the ball right to the middle?

There is something about the Pickleball game,
That strangers find rather silly;
For when I finally hit a great shot,
My partner shouts "Dilly, Dilly!"

There is something about the Pickleball game,
That whenever I attempt to dink;
I hit it too high, or into the net,
And wonder—*What did I think?*

There is something about the Pickleball game,
That demands a third shot drop;
But not matter how long or hard I try,
My result is often a flop.

There is something about the Pickleball game,
I enjoy playing with neighbor and friend;
But whether I win or whether I lose,
I'd like the game never to end!

FUN PLACES FOR PICKLEBALLERS TO VISIT AND DINE

Pickle Restaurant (Dublin, Ireland)

In A Pickle (Waltham, MA).

Fickle Pickle (Roswell, GA).

Pickles American Grill (Edmund, Moore, and Oklahoma City, OK)

Jacob's Pickle (New York City)

Mango Pickle Indian Bistro (Chicago)

Pig and Pickle (St. Louis, MO)

Purple Pickle Deli (Old Bridge, NJ)

Spicy Pickle (Denver, CO; Reno, NV)

Wooden Pickle (Marion, VA)

Maison Pickle (New York City)

Pickle Bar and Restaurant (Markle, IN)

D.B. Pickles (Ormond Beach, FL)

The Perfect Pickle (MN State Fair)

The Pickled Loon Saloon (Grand Rapids, MN)

The Pickle Factory (Vergas, MN)

Ye Old Pickle Factory (Nisswa, MN)

Bread & Pickle (Minneapolis, MN)

Pickles Café (Dunfee, IN) (Indianapolis, IN)

Pickles BBQ & Icehouse (Watauga, TX)

Pickle Tree Restaurant (Deerfield, WI)

Chicken N Pickle (Kansas City, KS) featuring on-site courts!

FUN WITH PICKLES
(a brief collection of unique and humorous terms)

PICKLEBALLER—Anyone who enjoys playing the game of pickleball and receives satisfaction from the sport.

PICKLEBILITY—The degree of skill that a specific pickleballer demonstrates.

PICKLED—The act of being held scoreless in a pickleball game (i.e., losing 0-11). (Some courts have an informal (and friendly) policy that pickled players must return home at the end of the session without their shirts on…)

PICKLEOCITY—The speed at which a pickleball travels at the moment of impact by one's paddle (possibly as high as 40 mph for professional players).

PICKLEPOWER—The multiplicative combination of the weight of a paddle times the strength of the player times the speed of the stroke to produce its effective overall force.

FICKLEPICKLE—The occasions on which the ball just won't go where the player aimed it (or hoped it would go). Also see UFE.

UFE—An UnForced Error; a shot hit wide, short, long, or that sets up an opponent's sharp volley or smash because of it being misshit, poorly aimed, too risky, etc. UnForced Errors ("UFERs") result in lost rallies and often lost points and lost games.

NET ABUSE—The act of a pickleballer unintentionally and repeatedly hitting the ball into (instead of over) the net, thus causing unnecessary wear and tear on the net and prematurely shortening its useful life.

FEEDING THE MONSTER—The act of (occasionally or repeatedly) accidentally feeding ("lifting") the pickleball to a strong opponent who then smashes the ball back at you for an easy winner.

LUCKY DUCK—The unintentionally evasive movement by a player when faced with a hard groundstroke or volley that then results in the opponent's ball sailing out of bounds without touching the defending player.

DILLED—The act of getting hit hard ("drilled" without the "r") somewhere on the body by an opponent's shot when failing to move quickly out of its way or hold one's paddle in a defensive location. (Dilled players often are heard to exclaim "Ouch!" or even a mild obscenity)

OBSESSIVE PICKLEBALL DISORDER (OPD)—A player's compulsion to play pickleball both frequently (e.g., multiple times per day or week) and for extended time periods (e.g., characterized by the repeated expression of "Just one more game"). This is also referred to as "pickleball addiction."

PICKLEBALL SHIRT SLOGANS

Almost everyone who has played pickleball on a few different courts has likely seen a wide variety of catchy slogans on the shirts of some players. In fact, numerous business organizations now offer a range of styles, colors, designs, and phrases on their products. Here is a sampling of these:

• Play pickleball—B Forever Young
• Dink responsibly
• Never underestimate an old man with a pickleball paddle
• Pickleball: Live the life
• Some grandmas knit scarves; real grandmas play pickleball
• Forecast: Sunny with a chance of pickleball
• Pickleball: My happy sport
• Pickleball: Dink, dink, dink, dink, SLAM
• Play pickleball
• Pickleball chick
• Let it bounce
• Retired: Therefore I play pickleball
• There's no crying in pickleball
• I dink and drive
• Pickleball rocks!
• I love pickleball
• I know; I know. Let it bounce!
• Pickleball is my happy place
• Live. Laugh. Play pickleball.
• Even a bad day of pickleball is better than NO day of pickleball
• Education is important, but pickleball is importanter
• O.P.D.—Obsessive Pickleball Disorder
• My grandma can beat your grandma at pickleball
• Pickleball queen
• Got pickleball?
• Pickleball legend
• Fear the paddle
• Pickleball: This is my happy hour
• Stay out of the kitchen; play pickleball

- I play like a girl, so try to keep up
- I love wine and pickleball
- Weekend forecast: Pickleball
- Paddles well with others
- I relish pickleball
- Body by pickleball
- Pickleball all day
- Retirement drives me to dink
- Ask me about my dinking problem
- Social Security, Medicare, & Pickleball: Life is good
- Great minds dink alike
- I swear…I was aiming for your feet!
- Pickleball University
- Pickleball—It's a dilly
- I'll take my bruises polka dotted
- Play pickleball; Be happy
- Keep calm and play pickleball
- I only wake up this early for pickleball
- Old pickleballers never die; they just dink around the kitchen
- I play pickleball. What's *your* superpower?
- Pickleball—the next Olympic sport
- I shall return
- Am I the one or the two?
- Straight up pickleballin'
- Patience before power
- A day without pickleball wouldn't kill me, but why risk it?
- All I care about is pickleball—and pizza
- I eat, sleep, and play pickleball
- Certified pickleball lover
- This pickleballer paddles well with others

PICKLE FOOD POSSIBILITIES

Background:

Just as this book's subtitle suggests that it will contain a smorgasbord of pickleball *topics*, gourmet diners may find great joy in creating and serving a smorgasbord of pickle-related *foods*. Guests could then pick and choose from among the items on a buffet table.

Alternatives:

Here is a sampling of the many possibilities that feature dill pickles:

- Dill pickle sandwiches
- Dill pickle soup
- Deep-fried dill pickles
- Dill pickle potato chips
- Dill pickle potato salad
- Dill pickle egg salad
- Beer batter fried pickles
- Dill pickle meatloaf
- Dill pickle pasta salad
- Dill pickle bread
- Pickle Dilly Snow Cone Syrup
- Archie McPhee Pickle Candy
- Dill Pickle Popcorn Seasoning
- Dee's Dill Pickle Flavored Peanuts
- Van Holten's Pickle Flavored Freeze Pops
- Vlasic Dill Pickle Sunflower Seeds
- Dill Pickle Lollipops
- Pickle Juice Sport Drink (for cramps)
- Pickle Juice Soda
- Pickle Candy Canes
- Gummi Pickles
- Farmhouse Culture Dill Pickle Kraut Krisps
- Twangerz Snack Topping Pickle Salt
- Best Maid Dill Juice
- Deep River Spicy Dill Pickle Snacks
- Emerald Dill Pickle Cashews

- Protein Krinkles Dill Pickles
- Doritos Intense Pickle Chips
- Oh Snap! Dilly Bites
- Pringles Screamin' Dill Pickle Potato Crisps

USEFUL PICKLEBALL EXCUSES

Pickleball players occasionally lose a point that they should have won, and teams sometimes lose games or even matches that they could have won. There are many common (and possibly acceptable) reasons for this problem, including Unforced Errors (discussed in Chapter 4), lack of adequate skill, temporary inattention, overall lack of focus, overconfidence, nervousness, or simply being outmatched by an opponent. Nevertheless, when explaining such a loss to a (probably disinterested) bystander or one's spouse/partner, it is often extremely useful to draw upon a previously developed reservoir of (hopefully) valid-*sounding* excuses, such as these:

"The sun was in my eyes."

"It was too windy."

"My opponents made bad line calls."

"The court seemed too short on their side."

"I thought my partner was going to hit it."

"My opponent poaches too much."

"My opponent uses a lot of topspin."

"My opponent puts sidespin on her serves."

"The net seems like it is too high."

"The new balls were too shiny and so they slid."

"I was using a new paddle and I'm not used to it yet."

"I borrowed a friend's paddle and it's totally different."

"My paddle seemed like it was too heavy today."

"My paddle has developed a dead spot."

"The referee was biased against us."

"My shoulder was sore from mowing my lawn."

"I got dehydrated and nearly fainted on the court."

"My partner missed way too many shots."

"I guess I shouldn't have signed up as a 5.0 player."

"I forgot my vitamins at home."

CHAPTER 8

Miscellaneous Topics

AVOIDING AND TREATING LEG CRAMPS*

What are they?
Leg cramps (also known as charley horses or spasms) are a common problem among many athletes, and pickleball players are also subject to them (especially in warm weather conditions or during/following extended periods of play). Cramps (sudden and painful tightening of certain muscles) can occur in one's calves, hamstrings, quadriceps, hands, or feet, lasting as long as 15 minutes and disrupting periods of sleep.

How do you avoid them?
Prevention is the best approach to leg cramps. Here are some suggestions:
1. Warm up your muscles first through light exercise, and *then* stretch your various muscle groups.
2. Know your physical limits and stick to them. Avoid the "just one more game" trap, and pace yourself. (Know when to say "No.")
3. Stay hydrated while playing and before. Even *without* exercising, medical experts recommend drinking 9 cups of liquid/day for women and 13 cups for men.
4. Increase your calcium intake by eating milk, cheese, yogurt, white beans, kale, sardines, salmon, or dried figs. Also consider taking calcium supplements (with vitamin D_3).
5. Take a magnesium supplement of about 400 mg/day, or eat more nuts and seeds.
6. Make sure that you get a sufficient amount of potassium (nearly 5,000 mg/day). Foods high in potassium include bananas, wholegrain breads, spinach, peanut butter, milk, and yogurt. Avoid or minimize diuretics.
7. Get a prescription for quinine (brand name Qualaquin).
8. Take an over-the-counter medication such as Hyland's Leg Cramp pills.
9. Take time to cool down after playing pickleball. Now is the time to go for a walk, or engage in gentle leg stretches.

10. Talk to your physician to make sure that you do not have an underlying condition causing cramps, such as diabetes, peripheral artery disease, thyroid disorders, liver malfunction, pregnancy, multiple sclerosis, alcoholism, or nerve disorders.
11. Avoid sitting for extended periods of time.

Treatment possibilities:
What can you do once you get leg cramps (*treatment*)?
1. Replenish your lost sodium from sweating. Eat salty food (i.e., pretzels, chips) and drink sports products that contain electrolytes. Eat a pickle or drink the juice from a pickle. Use large amounts of mustard.
2. Carefully consider your sleep position for your legs. Keep them straight; place a pillow under your calves. Let your feet dangle over the end of the bed.
3. Draw a bath of warm water (possibly with Epsom salts) and soak in it for several minutes. Alternatively, use a heating pad or even the application of ice or cold packs (separated from your skin by a towel).

*Note: Much of this information is drawn from Internet sources.

THE "OVER AND BACK" RULE IN PICKLEBALL

The governing rule.

One of the little-known and somewhat unique rules in pickleball that is rarely explained during introductory training classes concerns a ball that has been hit over the net and then returns back over it again *without having been hit by the other team*. This is governed by Rule 11.I.1. of the 2018 USAPA/IFP "Official Tournament Rulebook," which reads as follows:

"If the ball bounces into a player's non-volley zone with enough backspin as to cause it to return over the net, the player may reach over or around the net to hit the ball but may not touch the net system or the opponent's court."

Note that if you fail to initiate contact and play a direct role in returning the ball to your opponents' court, you will have *lost* the point.

Two clarifications.

Since rules are sometimes difficult to understand, some explanation is in order. First, a non-returned ball of this nature may actually be the result of two (not just one) factors—not only a *high degree of backspin* applied by your opponent, but also simply from a *strong wind behind you*. (Note that the latter factor happens only when playing outdoors.) The second point needing clarification is that the ball doesn't need to have bounced only in your non-volley zone before this rule applies; it could have bounced in any portion of your entire court. The rule is clear, however, that the receiving team must make contact with the ball *before* it hits the other team's court (even as it is blowing or spinning away from you).

How do you successfully accomplish this feat?
Here are some suggestions:
1. *Know the rule*, and be prepared to explain it if it occurs.
2. Be prepared (especially on a windy day) and *anticipate that this situation may occur* when the wind is against your back. In other words, having either watched your opponent's previous use of backspin, or having observed the wind's effect on balls lobbed toward you on a very

breezy day, you can predict that this event may occur and thus begin moving forward to place yourself in a position closer to the net than usual. (Remember, you *may* enter the NVZ at *any* time, not just after a ball has bounced within it.)

3. *Strike the ball before it has re-crossed the net*, if possible. Although the ball is now moving away from you (in sharp contrast to most volley exchanges), you can now add your own impact to its own velocity to hit a really powerful shot. Just be careful that you don't hit it too far and don't make contact with the net!

4. *Contact the ball after it has re-crossed the net.* You will need to reach over the net to do this. You may try to hit the ball a) *forward* (toward your opponents), b) angled sharply *sideways* (to make it difficult for them to get to the ball), c) *downward* (e.g., by lightly tapping or tipping the ball so that it "dies" very quickly in the opponents' court), or d) by the extremely difficult attempt to hit it *backwards* (toward you) into the net.

In any event, be prepared to laugh at yourself or (with) your opponents as you all experience one of the stranger occurrences in pickleball!

ROLE OF THE REFEREE

Absence of a referee

Recreational (social) pickleball games rarely need (or use) a referee. Instead, players make all their own calls based on honesty, good will, trust, and sportsmanship. Most differences of opinion are thereby resolved amicably.

Presence of a referee

Tournament play is different, since the outcomes of a match may affect player ratings, the prestige of the players, and even the amount of prize money (for professional players). Under tournament conditions it is helpful and necessary to have both a referee and four line judges to assist the referee (one for each baseline and one for each sideline). A rigorous formal program for educating and certifying new referees is available & conducted by representatives of the USAPA.

Role of a referee

What does a referee do? When referees are present in tournament games, they are responsible for all decisions related to procedural and judgment calls during a match. Prior to a match, referees check on court and net conditions, the supply of balls, scorecards, and a clock, and meet with players to introduce them to each other, inspect their paddles, emphasize waiting for the score to be called before serving, instruct players on the roles of line judges and players, and introduce some fair method of determining initial service and side of the court. The referee also notes who is the starting server on each team for each game.

During a game itself, referees are responsible for keeping score, monitoring time, mediating disputes, and enforcing the rules. They call the score (and mark their scorecard) after each point has been played, call baseline foot faults on the serve, service violations, and NVZ infractions, monitor time outs, observe player positions for accuracy, and handle appeals from players relating to line calls. Their role is to keep the game moving while assuring fairness to all participants.

Referees do not normally make line calls except under two combined conditions. First, a referee may make a judgment if one team *appeals* a call (e.g., a line call) by the other team. Second, a referee should only intervene if the referee clearly *saw* the ball hit the court.

Requirements

Referees need to have a comprehensive grasp of pickleball rules so they can make accurate and fair judgments. They are also responsible for ensuring safety by stopping play if a stray ball enters the court. Referees have total control of the court, and they monitor unsportsmanlike conduct, clear rule violations, unnecessary delays of the game, and (disallowed) coaching from the sidelines. They may issue technical warnings and technical fouls for egregious behavior.

Conclusion

Learn to trust and respect your referee, but don't hesitate to question his or her interpretation of the rules or accuracy of the score. If necessary, you may appeal a referee's decision to the tournament director.

RALLY SCORING FOR PICKLEBALL

Scoring Confusion

Pickleball scoring is somewhat unique. As a result, the scoring system for pickleball games can be a little tricky for instructors to teach, and often times new players are initially confused by the combinations of the three numbers (e.g., "our score, their score, and server number 1 or 2"). Confusion even occasionally reigns on the court among more experienced players, as evidenced by conversations around the questions of "Whose serve is it?" or "What is the correct score?" or "Am I server number one or server number two?" or "Who was the "start" server in this game?"

A Borrowed Alternative

To combat this confusion, some interest has recently arisen among a small set of pickleballers nationwide who are advocating a change to *rally scoring*. The beauty of rally point scoring lies in its simplicity, as the side (team) that wins each *rally* scores one point. In addition, the side that wins a point also immediately wins the right to serve the next one, thus doubling the importance of each point.

Rationales

Why do some players want rally scoring?

1. Advocates of rally scoring assert that games using rally scoring are completed much faster (e.g., by 20-30%). As a result of speedier games, players on the sidelines get back onto the courts much sooner. They don't lose interest, and they don't stiffen up from lack of movement.

2. In addition, the simplistic scoring system only uses two numbers ("Our score vs. your score") and does not require remembering server numbers (since the loss of a point dictates loss of serve for that team). The other team then will serve from the right side if their score is even, or the left side if their score is odd. In doubles play, each partner may be allowed to serve until he/she loses a point. Players

on a team only switch sides on their court if they make a point while serving.

3. Another rationale for rally scoring is that other sports (e.g. badminton, table tennis, and volleyball) already use this simplified system of points, and therefore it is familiar to participants and spectators alike all around the world. If games played to 11 points are completed *too* rapidly under rally scoring, the standard game could be set at 15 or 21 with the game ending when one team reaches that level (and is ahead by two).

The Immediate Prospects

The USAPA has officially rejected the proposed change to rally scoring at this time. Until the issue is raised again, individual players in local settings or even club tournaments could begin experimenting with rally scoring to see whether or not they like it. Finally, the other remaining impediment to converting the scoring system lies in the difficulty of implementing the change for the several million players who have the existing system embedded in their minds and regular systems of play. Resistance to change often rules the day!

PICKLEBALL'S "SKINNY SINGLES" GAME*

The vast majority of pickleball games, both recreationally and competitively (in tournaments) are played as *doubles*. This, of course, requires the presence of at least four persons to be present. The doubles format also presents its own unique elements and strategies and challenges (i.e., hitting to the middle, partner communication, "stacking").

Normal singles games.
The obvious alternative, especially if only two persons are available to practice or play, is the classic *full-court singles* format, in which the two competing players use the entire pickleball court (as opposed to tennis, where the court is shrunk for singles matches), serves are made diagonally, and players alternate between left and right sides depending on their current score. However, this requires more active movement by the players to cover the entire court and thus tests or wears out their stamina more rapidly.

Skinny singles.
Another alternative is called *skinny singles* (or half-court singles, or small singles), in which the entire game is played on only one side of the centerline (left side, or right side) of the full court. This format has recently been used in tournament play (e.g., the 2017 Wisconsin Cup) as well as for skill practice sessions—especially when only two persons are available. Players make their serves straight ahead and their opponent returns serves straight ahead. Players have the opportunity for intense practice of accurate serves, returns, the "third shot drop," dinks, and volleys, (as well as occasional lobs and lob returns). A premium is placed on accurate shot placement (as the target area has now shrunk from 20 feet wide to 10 feet wide) and distance control. Games can be played to 11 points (win by 2), or shortened to 5 or 7 or 9 points.

Skinny singles can also be played *diagonally,* where each player serves to the far service court (e.g., NW to SE, or NE to SW), and each player defends *their* respective side of the court. (Any ball not hit diagonally into the appropriate court is a fault.)

This provides more realistic practice of serving for normal (doubles) play, and more practice of angled shots.

A combination of the two skinny singles designs is to have the players serve diagonally but then continue to play only on the *receiver's* side of the court. In this approach, servers would alternate serving from the left or right side, depending on their score (even or odd).

*Material for this description has been drawn from a variety of sources, including statements by Aspen Kern, Sarah Ansboury, Coach "Mo," Kyle Yates, and Jordan Briones (see: *http://jbrish.com/skinny-pickleball-what/*).

(SELF) REVIEW OF PB RULES: TRUE OR FALSE?

For each question below, indicate whether you believe the statement to be correct (True) or incorrect (False).

1. It is OK for a player standing outside the court to catch an opponent's shot (in the air) and then call it "Out."
2. A serve that strikes the receiver's partner results in a replay.
3. When hitting the ball, the arm above the wrist (e.g., up to the elbow) is considered part of the paddle.
4. It is a violation of the rules for the server to bounce the ball several times and then serve it out of his/her hand.
5. You must wait until a ball lands in the NVZ before you can enter the zone to return a ball.
6. A player who successfully volleys a shot but then accidentally drops his/her paddle into the NVZ is guilty of a "Fault."
7. A served ball that lands on the NVZ line is considered a "Fault."
8. If neither the receiver nor his/her partner saw a shot clearly enough to call it "In" or "Out" it should be replayed.
9. If the receiver and his/her partner disagree on whether a shot was "In" or "Out" then it should be ruled as "Out."
10. A ball that is lobbed over the net but then spins back over the net before being touched by the receiving team is a valid point for the team that last hit the ball (if they had initially served it).
11. A "rally" and a "volley" are interchangeable terms; they essentially mean the same thing.
12. Foot faults at the NVZ line can be called by any of the four players In a doubles game.
13. The "Oh Oh" shot is a legitimate way to avoid having a point count against your team.
14. Rally scoring appears poised to replace the existing pickleball scoring system in the near future.

15. "Bookmaking" is an acceptable method for cataloging opponent weaknesses.

A BRIEF GUIDE TO SOURCES ON PICKLEBALL

2018 Official Tournament Rulebook, by USAPA & IFP

Pickleball: Less is More, by Pat Carroll

A Pickleball Playbook: A Guide for Instructors and Self-Instruction, by James Valleskey

Pickleball Fundamentals, by USAPA with Mary Littlewood

Mind Game: A Quantum Performance Leap for Competitive Pickleball and Tennis, by Neil P. Schulenburg

The Art of Pickleball: Strategies and Techniques for Everyone, by Gale H. Leach

Smart Pickleball: The Pickleball Guru's Guide, by Prem Carnot & Wendy Garrido

Pickleball Zen: The Inner Game, by Paul Hudanich

Pickleball 5.0: A Journey from 2.0 to 5.0, by Phil Dunmeyer

At the Line Pickleball: The Winning Doubles Pickleball Strategy, by Joe Baker

The Pickleball Bible: Student Edition, by Rick Lamson and Tim Finger

History of Pickleball: More than 50 Years of Fun, by Jennifer Lucore and Beverly Youngren

Pickleball CPR Drills: Coaching Pickleball Readiness, by Claudia A. Fontana

Pickleball Supremacy: Practical Pickleball Blueprint, by Solanna Adams and JetGripz

Never Underestimate an Old Man with a Pickleball Paddle: Pickleball Player Writing Journal Lined, Diary, Notebook, by Not Only Journals

Target Zones: Practicing Pickleball with Purpose, by Diane Ahern and Lisa Duncan

The Official Pickleball Handbook, by Mark Friedenberg

SEE ALSO VISUAL INSTRUCTIONAL AIDS SUCH AS:

Pickleball Clinics by Coach Mo: Strategies and Techniques

Pickleball Clinics DVS with Bonus Lessons

The Ultimate Pickleball Instructional DVD, by Dennis Forbes

Pickleball: Improve Your Game, by Alan Christensen

Pickleball Courts: A Construction & Maintenance Manual

Made in the USA
Las Vegas, NV
01 December 2021

35804903R00098